OUR DIVINE PARENT

Our Divine Parent

A Biblical Theology of the Family of God

JOSHUA JOEL SPOELSTRA

WIPF & STOCK · Eugene, Oregon

OUR DIVINE PARENT
A Biblical Theology of the Family of God

Wipf & Stock
An Imprint of Wipf and Stock Publishers
199 W. 8th Ave., Suite 3
Eugene, OR 97401

www.wipfandstock.com

PAPERBACK ISBN: 978-1-7252-6762-6
HARDCOVER ISBN: 978-1-7252-6761-9
EBOOK ISBN: 978-1-7252-6763-3

Manufactured in the U.S.A. JULY 9, 2020

Dedication

To Rosalind, Anastasia, and Lily Mae

children are a gift from the LORD;
the fruit of the womb is a divine reward.
(Psalm 127:3, CEB)

Contents

Abbreviations

ABD	David Noel Freedman, ed. *Anchor Bible Dictionary*. 6 vols. New York: Doubleday, 1992.
BCE	before Common Era
BDAG	Danker, Frederick William, et al., eds. *A Greek-English Lexicon of the New Testament and other Early Christian Literature*. 3rd ed. Chicago: University of Chicago Press, 2000.
BDB	Brown, Francis, et al. *Hebrew and English Lexicon of the Old Testament with an Appendix Containing the Biblical Aramaic*. Peabody, MA: Hendrickson, 2006.
CE	Common Era
Gk.	Greek
Heb.	Hebrew
HALOT	Koehler, Ludwig, and Walter Baumgartner. *The Hebrew and Aramaic Lexicon of the Old Testament*, 2 vols. London: Brill, 2001.
IBD	Douglas, J.D. and N. Hillyer, eds. *The Illustrated Bible Dictionary*. 3 vols. Wheaton, IL: Tyndale, 1980.

TDNT	Gerhard Kittel, ed. *Theological Dictionary of the New Testament*. 10 vols. Grand Rapids: Eerdmans, 1964.
USB4	United Bible Society. *The Greek New Testament*. 4th rev. ed. Stuttgart: Deutsche Bibelgesellschaft, 2001.

Introduction

Topic, Thesis, and Scope

ARISTOTLE AND PLATO ONCE philosophized that the abolition of families, as well as implementing other changes, would give way to create the ideal society.[1] Now, over twenty-three centuries later, the family unit is still a vital institution in most, if not all, societies around the world. Nevertheless, the family unit has witnessed many different configurations over time, which seems to attest to its significance and resilience.

The contemporary familial landscape includes traditional expressions of family units; also, there are mixed/blended/joint families, multiracial families, and transnational families. Parents may be comprised of opposite-sex or same-sex spouses, the single parent or the guardian(s). Children of a family may be biological, adopted, or fosterlings. The family-by-choice option may comprise distant relatives and/or nonbiological persons, such as friends or partners. A nuclear and/or extended family may feel broken or whole, fractured or nurturing, estranging or accepting; indeed, family can be a prison or a haven, or any experience in-between.

Another layer of familial relationality, moreover, is the phenomenon of spiritual family, whether this is understood generally as fellow adherents of a religion/faith or cognized in more specific filial terms; further, spiritual family may or may not overlay or

1. Aristotle, *Pol.* 2.1–5; Plato, *Rep.* 5.

intersect with biological family. In Christianity, the entire Bible portrays the metaphorical story of the family of God as a present reality and a progressive revelation. This book encapsulates a fresh approach to the broad subject of the family of God, according to Scripture's mosaic, which saliently elucidates the intentions of God for relationship and belonging, purpose and fulfillment for humankind.

To be sure, there are many literary works whose scope focuses on one aspect or a complex of issues related to the family of God. For instance, there is a growing body of literature committed to gender and sexuality and God in theological scholarship;[2] some treatises even construct God as a father[3] or mother.[4] Additionally, child/children studies is a rising socio-scientific interest emerging in the field of biblical studies.[5] There are also numerous volumes concerning one particular function of the family of God, as viewed in the Bible, such as adoption.[6] The current work, alternatively, integrates many elements encompassing each entity of the divine family unit; it incorporates the major functions and important ancillary aspects of the family of God. Occasionally, an integrative presentation is put forth; yet, it is usually within the limited scope of a biblical book (e.g., Isaiah, John) or corpus (e.g., Pauline Epistles, Prophets).[7] In spite of this, a holistic treatment

2. Sawyer, *God, Gender and the Bible*; Thatcher, *God, Sex, and Gender*; cf. also Soskice, *Kindness of God*; Løland, *Silent Or Salient Gender?*; Maier, *Daughter Zion, Mother Zion*.

3. Miller, *Biblical Faith and Fathering*; Wright, *Knowing God the Father*. Cf. Besançon Spencer, "Father-Ruler," 433–42; Niskanen, "Yhwh as Father, Redeemer, and Potter," 397–407; Dille, *Mixing Metaphors*.

4. Smith, *God "Mother"*; Meehan, *Feminine Divine*; Mollenkott, *Divine Feminine*. Cf. Dille, *Mixing Metaphors*; Claassens, *Mourner, Mother, Midwife*.

5. E.g., Fretheim and Gaventa, *Child in the Bible*; Flynn, *Children in Ancient Israel*; Flynn, *Children in the Bible*; Garroway and Martens, *Children and Methods*; Betsworth and Parker, *Handbook of Children*.

6. E.g., Heim, *Adoption*; Lewis, *Paul's 'Spirit of Adoption'*; Scott, *Adoption*; Burke, *Adopted*.

7. E.g., Darr, *Isaiah's Vision*; Dille, *Mixing Metaphors*; Løland, *Silent Or Salient Gender?*; Howard-Brook, *Becoming Children of God*; Watt, *Family of the King*; Burke, *Adopted*; Heim, *Adoption*; Lewis, *Paul's 'Spirit of Adoption'*;

of the biblical metaphor of the family of God spanning the whole Christian Bible is necessitous.

In short, the trajectory of integrated entities and aspects of the family of God are as follows. God is a Divine Parent; God, in the Bible, is not only portrayed in terms and quality both as a father but also as a mother. The Divine Parent, also, has progeny. Israel is portrayed (collectively) as a son and, alternatively, also as a daughter; moreover, Jesus as the very child of God exhibits, and is the template for, perfect relationship with the Divine Parent. Thus, a family unity exists with the Divine Parent and child(ren) of God—and this is the family of God. Furthermore, God loves orphans and engages in adoption; through the adoption price of Jesus' life and the security deposit of the Holy Spirit, God purchases (redeems) estranged/orphaned children for God's eternal/divine family through regeneration by the Holy Spirit upon faith in Jesus the Christ. As siblings of and co-heirs with Christ Jesus, discipleship into the fullness of Jesus Christ is illustrated as spiritual parenting (disciple-makers) and maturing spiritual children (those being discipled). In the end, God's loved children are to grow up into Christ, the true elder brother, and emulate the Divine Parent in all things and in all ways.

Presuppositions and Hypotheses

Two main presuppositions must be registered which undergird the thesis that God is a Divine Parent of the family of God, comprising human children. One hypothesis involves the image of God as an interpretive crux; inherent to humankind, the *imago Dei* conjoins God and people in some meaningful way. Also, observing that most verbiage regarding the "Divine Parent" or the "child of God" is present in poetic sections of the Hebrew Bible, the second hypothesis submitted is that the New Testament makes typological use of Old Testament metaphors. Each presupposition shall be elaborated.

Peppard, "Adopted and Begotten"; Scott, *Adoption*; Sampley, *Paul in the Greco-Roman World*.

Image of God: The Interpretive Crux for God as Parent and Humankind as Children

The image of God (Gen 1:27) is the crux of interpretation for the hermeneutical foundation of God as parent and humanity as children, for it is the first and most instructive instance which informs this framework. Indeed, the *imago Dei* reveals the gendered diversity of humankind and its relational and procreative capacities. Thus, Genesis 1:26–28 is paradigmatic for the conception of God as Divine Parent (father and mother); and God's children are males and females (literal of humanity), sons and daughters (metaphorical of personified Israel).

In Genesis 1, near the end of all the creative works of God, God creates humankind. God prefaces this creation with the following purpose and intention. "'Let us make humanity in our image to resemble us . . . ' [So] God created humanity in God's own image, in the divine image God created them, male and female God created them" (Gen 1:26–27, CEB). Germane for our purposes is the correspondence between the plurality yet singularity of God (triunity)[8] and the plurality yet singularity of humanity (male and female),[9] and its implications for the human species.[10]

By virtue of humankind sharing in God's image and likeness, maleness and femaleness both resemble God to some extent. Implicit in this passage is the concept that God transcends gender

8. I operate under the assumption that God is a triunity, Trinity. In Genesis 1:1–3, God is acknowledged (v. 1) as well as the Spirit of God (v. 2); and when God speaks (v. 3) this evokes another entity of the Triune God, according to the New Testament. Of Jesus the Christ, it is acclaimed: "In the beginning was the Word, and the Word was with God, and the Word was God. He was in the beginning with God. All things came into being through him, and without him not one thing came into being" (John 1:1–3, NRSV). As a result, the pre-incarnate Messiah may be viewed as the mouthpiece of creation (cf. Col 1:16).

9. Keiser, *Divine Plural*, 141.

10. Soskice, *Kindness of God*, 49: "The as yet unsung glory of Gen. 1:26–7 is that the fullness of divine life and creativity is reflected by a human race which is male and female, which encompasses if not an ontological then a primal difference."

(cf. Isa 55:9), yet somehow also encompasses gender;[11] therefore, something of God is revealed in/through human gender. Furthermore, "the [biblical] text's presentation of the plurality of humanity in terms of sexual diversity in some manner reflects something of the unity in the plurality of God."[12] Indeed, even humanity's sexuality is a reflection or expression of the image of God, ostensibly; for, as the triune God creates, so similarly does humanity procreate.[13]

It is precisely when the original humans procreate, in fact, where the verbiage of one being in the image and likeness of another is registered next in the Bible. The filial dimension of the image of God comes into focus bi-optically when Genesis 1:26–27 is viewed together with Genesis 5:1–3.

> When God created humankind, he made them in the likeness of God. Male and female he created them, and he blessed them and named them 'Humankind' when they were created. When Adam had lived one hundred thirty years, he became the father of a son in his likeness, according to his image, and named him Seth. (Gen 5:1–3, NRSV)

Image (Heb. *ṣelem*) and likeness (Heb. *dəmût*) are utilized in both Genesis 1 and 5 to convey: "As Adam is Seth's father, so too God is the parent of humanity."[14] "In this context," in other words, "it is explicit that the resemblance between God and humanity

11. So McGregor Wright, "God, Metaphor and Gender," 287–300. Contra de Moor, who states: "The poetical structure of Gen 1:27 clearly suggests that God himself too was both male and female" ("Duality in God and Man," 122). Mollenkott (*Divine Feminine*, 21), relatedly, surmises, "God . . . is simultaneously *both* male and female, and *neither* male nor female." (emphasis original)

12. Keiser, *Divine Plural*, 137.

13. Bird, "Male and Female," 146–50, 157–59. McDowell (*Image of God*, 125) maintains, this "correspondence is intrinsic to being human and is passed on by the parents, who themselves are created in the image and likeness of God, to their children at birth."

14. Crouch, "Humanity's Divine Parentage," 10. There exists "a parallel between the father-son relationship of 5:3, between Adam and Seth, and the divine-human relationship of 1:26–7 and 5:1" (Crouch, "Humanity's Divine Parentage," 10).

is analogous to the resemblance between a parent and child."[15] In fact, Deuteronomy 32:6 and Malachi 2:10 both refer to God as creator and father, which mirrors the language of Genesis 1. Consequently, Genesis 1:27 and 5:1–3 is paradigmatic to speak of humankind as the children of God, and God as Divine Parent.[16]

God is often depicted in Scripture in anthropomorphic terms, and this is done so that humans might better understand God.[17] However, if humankind is created in the image of God, then it seems more appropriate to speak of humans in theomorphic terms—as image bearers of God.[18] Stated differently, God is not made according to human form, but humans (anthro-) are made according to the form (morph-) of God (theo-). So rather than (merely) focusing on language which portrays God with human body parts or mental faculties, etc., it is sage to interpret the social, physical, emotional, and spiritual capacities, etc. of humans, as resonances and reflections of God in/through humanity.[19] Moreover, it is when the genders live in harmony and equity that God is most accurately represented,[20] for God—who is (three in) one—lives in perfect community with Godself.

15. Knafl, *Forming God*, 65; cf. also McDowell, *Image of God*, 125.

16. McDowell, *Image of God*, 131–32, 133–34.

17. Thus, neither the notion of *God as mother* nor *God as father* is an effort to make God a female/woman or a male/man.

18. Knafl (*Forming God*, 126) explains: "While it is of course true that Gen 1:26–27 presents what has been called a theomorphic conception of the human form, this should not be considered antithetical to an anthropomorphic conception of the divine form."

19. Relatedly, humanity's qualities represent in limited capacity God's own qualities (as presented in the Bible); these are called communicable attributes. God also has incommunicable attributes, aspects of Godself which are not shared with humankind; these include omnipresence (all-present), omniscience (all-knowing), omnipotence (all-powerful), immutability (never-changing), and immortality (although, immortality does come to light in the resurrection of Jesus [Rom 2:7; 1 Cor 15:53–54; 2 Tim 1:10]). See further any systematic theology book.

20. Horowitz ("Is Woman Included?," 204) notes, "from the Talmudic rabbis, one learns that man and woman need one another to participate fully in the image of God." Cf. Hess, "Equality With and Without Innocence," 79–95; Soskice, *Kindness of God*, 49–51. See further Wijk-Bos, *Reimagining God*,

Poetic Biblical Literature: The Vehicle for Familial Terms and Its Subsidiary Relationships

Another exegetical phenomenon which undergirds the presupposition of constructing a biblical portrait of a Divine Parent who forms the family of God is the fact that most of the complex terms and images derive from biblical literature whose genre is poetic. More accentuated than the nonfigurative style of narrative, poetry is the vehicle for figurative language, including metaphor. Throughout the Old Testament's poetic sections, chiefly, God is depicted as a parent of a child.

God as a father is a metaphor found in Psalms and Proverbs, which are part of the Wisdom Literature marked by its poetic language in prayers and aphorisms. Also, the *father* pseudonym is present in the Song of Moses (Deut 32). Even the dialogues and diatribes of the prophets have a quality of poetry; this is the case, for example, with Isaiah, Jeremiah, and Malachi.

God as a mother is a metaphor also found in Psalms, Proverbs, and the Song of Moses (Deut 32). Motherly aspects of God feature in the stanzaic speech of God in Job 38, and the same is subtly present in the creation poem/hymn of Genesis 1. In addition, Isaiah's oracles are suffused with feminine imagery of God.

Interestingly, God as both a mother and a father are interchangeable metaphors found in the same biblical book,[21] and even in the same verse (Deut 32:18). God siring (father aspect) and birthing (mother aspect) Israel conjures another metaphorical matrix, namely an asexual reproduction via parthenogenesis (the process of creating offspring from one parent). Ultimately, God as mother and/or father is a metaphorical means in the Bible to acclaim God as the sole source of all life.

The child of God is portrayed in nonliteral biblical literature as both a son and a daughter. The metaphor of Israel as a son is part of prophetic speeches (Hosea and Jeremiah) and a divine speech (2 Sam 7; 1 Chr 17). Daughter Israel is a metaphor utilized

23–26; Stiebert, *Fathers and Daughters*, 176–85.

21. Dille, *Mixing Metaphors*; Wijk-Bos, *Reimagining God*.

in Ezekiel; alternatively, Daughter Zion is a moniker appropriated in Isaiah, Jeremiah, Lamentations, Micah, Zephaniah, and Zechariah, as well as the Psalms. These corpora all lend themselves to the figurative use of linguistics.

The New Testament, on the other hand, does not comprise as much poetic literature; nonetheless, the terminology of God as a parent and the church as God's children is more expansively attested. Apparently, that which is figurative in the Old Testament transforms into typology in the New Testament. Scriptural typology is, as F. F. Bruce states,

> [a] way of setting forth the biblical history of salvation so that some of its earlier phases are seen as anticipations of latter phases, or some later phase as the recapitulation or fulfilment of an early one. . . . In the language of typology, the earlier series of events constituted a 'type' of the latter; the latter series was an 'antitype' of the earlier. Or it may be said that the successive epochs of salvation-history disclose a recurring pattern of divine activity which the NT writers believed to have found its definitive expression in their own day.[22]

Consequently, Jesus in the Gospels and the apostles in the Epistles speak and write prolifically in terms of the household of faith, the family of God, being born of God, being children of God, being sons and daughters of God in Christ by the Spirit, etc.; further, spiritual adoption, spiritual parentage and progeny, and relationships amongst spiritual siblings is commonly articulated in the New Testament.

Therefore, the "Divine Parent" and "child(ren) of God" metaphor is most often found in the poetic portions of the Old Testament, whether in poemic utterances or prophetic oracles; yet this is to be expected, since poetry is nonliteral language which can stimulate human imagination. New Testament typological expressions of the Divine Parent and family of God harness the figurative and metaphoric language of the Old Testament, typifying salvation-relationship with the Triune God. Consequently,

22. Bruce, "Typology," 3:1602.

matters of divine parentage and childhood relationships, etc., are the experiences of life in Christ by the Spirit of God.

Methodology and Approach

In order to substantiate the previous presuppositions and hypotheses, and to judiciously proceed in the present investigation, interpretative methodologies must be established to undergird and guide exegesis. In that vein, a biblical theology of the family of God through conceptual metaphor theory is a fitting approach for the current subject and study. These exegetical methods will be briefly explained and their goal(s) shown.

Conceptual Metaphor Theory

Though metaphors are mostly couched in literature whose genre is poetry they are not exclusively a poetic or rhetorical device; rather, metaphors are conceptually based, and are therefore present in narrative too.[23] Catalyzed by the seminal work of George Lakoff and Mark Johnson,[24] Conceptual Metaphor Theory is a fruitful field of study impacting biblical studies.[25] "The standard definition of . . . *A conceptual metaphor is understanding one domain of experience (that is typically abstract) in terms of another (that is typically concrete).*"[26]

These two realms are typically termed the target domain and source domain;[27] the former is the unknown or abstract which is

23. Hampe, "Embodiment and Discourse," 4.

24. Lakoff and Johnson, *Metaphors We Live By.*

25. E.g., DesCamp, *Metaphor and Ideology*; Heim, *Adoption*; Shead, *Radical Frame Semantics*; Watt, *Family of the King*; Dille, *Mixing Metaphors*; Feyaerts, *Bible through Metaphor and Translation*; Soskice, *Kindness of God.*

26. Kövecses, "Conceptual Metaphor Theory," 13 (italics original). This definition "can be reformulated somewhat more technically as . . . *A conceptual metaphor is a systematic set of correspondences between two domains of experience*" (Kövecses, "Conceptual Metaphor Theory," 14; italics original).

27. Kövecses, "Conceptual Metaphor Theory," 16.

sought to be understood by the know or concrete repertoire of experience. The matter of directionality between target and source domains is critical, because if misapplied the meaning and theology becomes skewed. For example, "God is Father" is a metaphor which seeks to understand God through the metaphorical grid of a human father role (source → target); however, "Father is God" erroneously values a human father as a deity (source ← target).[28] In the Bible, consequently, the target is to understand God (the abstract) from the known, natural, and physical domain of general revelation; and, specific to the present purposes, Divine-human relationship is metaphorically rendered as the family of God.

There are other figurative types of language that feature in the present work, additionally. Under the umbrella of metaphor is personification; frequently appropriated in the Bible, personification is a device to collectively refer to a city or people group as a single personage.[29] Similarly, simile is not too unlike metaphor;[30] in this book the chapter titles are technically similes, yet the same general function of nonliteral, metaphorical language is presumed. Finally, the mechanics of Conceptual Metaphor Theory operate here within the larger framework of biblical theology.

Biblical Theology

"Biblical Theology," writes Geerhardus Vos, "deals with the process of the self-revelation of God deposited in the Bible."[31] Furthermore, biblical theology appreciates that God's revelation is progressive—namely, God discloses redemption history beautifully and cyclically throughout time until ultimately redemption is embodied in the Son of God, Jesus Christ.[32] Thus,

28. Cf. Sweetser and DesCamp, "Motivating Biblical Metaphors for God," 20–22.

29. Maier, *Daughter Zion, Mother Zion*, 17–28.

30. See Løland's discussion on metaphor and simile (*Silent Or Salient Gender?*, 47-51).

31. Vos, *Biblical Theology*, 5.

32. Vos, *Biblical Theology*, 3–18.

> biblical theology may be defined as theological interpretation of Scripture in and for the church. It proceeds with historical and literary sensitivity and seeks to analyze and synthesize the Bible's teaching about God and his relations to the world on its own terms, maintaining sight of the Bible's overarching narrative and Christocentric focus.[33]

Contrastive somewhat with systematic theology, which synchronically categorizes Scripture into various subject, "biblical theology has had a strong diachronic strain that insists on tracing the historic development of doctrine as it appeared chronologically in the history of Israel and the church."[34] Consequently, the trajectory and contour of biblical themes and the development and tensions of scriptural motifs are not problematic—but rather expected—in biblical theology, as opposed to the somewhat monolithic presentation that systematic theology intonates.[35]

Since biblical theology understands Christ as the climax of revelation, historically and redemptively, it therefore assumes, or subsumes, canonical criticism.[36] Canonical criticism values the cohesive message of the entire (Christian) Bible and seeks to demonstrate the unity and consistency of God's revelation and saving activity in both the Old and New Testaments.[37] Once Jesus fulfills the Law, Prophets, and Writings (cf. Luke 24:44–48), the christologically salvific-redemptive move of God exponentially extends to envelope larger portions of humanity.

Klink and Lockett, in their book *Understanding Biblical Theology*, have offered a helpful spectrum by which to cognize the

33. Alexander and Rosner, *New Dictionary of Biblical Theology*, 10 (original passage wholly in italics, removed here for clarity).

34. Kaiser, *Promise-Plan*, 18.

35. Cf. Mead, *Biblical Theology*; Walsh and Elliott, *Biblical Theology*.

36. Klink and Lockett, *Understanding Biblical Theology*, 125–53; Childs, *Biblical Theology*, 70–79.

37. See Noble, *Canonical Approach*.

various hues and emphases within the disciple of biblical theology; their graph is reconstructed here.[38]

HISTORY..........THEOLOGY				
Type 1	Type 2	Type 3	Type 4	Type 5
Historical Description	History of Redemption	Worldview–Story	Canonical Approach	Theological Construction

These types of biblical theology are not antithetical or irreconcilable one to another; instead, each finds itself compatibly on a continuum somewhere between the two poles. In this book, while each of the five types is assumed and developed to some extent, the specific methodological perspective of biblical theology herein is a worldview-story approach,[39] through the theme of the family of God.[40] Accordingly, the reader is invited to behold the Bible's metanarrative of *Our Divine Parent* and the family of God—even to adopt its scriptural worldview and actively participate in God's unfolding story!

Outline of Chapters

Initially, the Divine Parent is analyzed in Scripture in terms of being rendered as a father (chapter 1) and a mother (chapter 2). Subsequently, God's child is, in the Old Testament, alternatively portrayed as a son (chapter 3) and a daughter (chapter 4). The divine family expands by means of spiritual adoption, in the New Testament (chapter 5); and growing and maturing (discipleship) into the Christ of God by the Spirit of God, along with interpersonal relationships within and outside the household of God, are explored (chapter 6).

38. Klink and Lockett, *Understanding Biblical Theology*, 22.

39. See Klink and Lockett, *Understanding Biblical Theology*, 93–122; Brown, "Biblical Theology Story-Shaped?," 13–31.

40. Cf. Hafemann and House, *Central Themes in Biblical Theology*; cf. also Wells, *God's Holy People*.

1

God as Father

It is well-known, and oft-lamented, that the Bible is thoroughly patriarchal—even androcentric—in orientation.[1] Notwithstanding, the biblical language of God as father is *metaphoric*;[2] metaphoric also is the biblical literature when casting God as mother (chapter 2). Consequently, it is worthwhile investigating how God relates to humans not only generally as a male/man but specifically through the familial metaphor of father.[3]

In this chapter, the few references to God as father in the Old Testament are examined, initially; it is in the New Testament, conversely, where prolific attestation to divine fatherhood exists, whether vocalized by Jesus in the Gospels,[4] especially John,[5] or by

1. Cf. Childs, *Old Testament Theology*, 39–42.

2. D'Angelo ("Intimating Deity," 63) nuances: "for the ancient theologian (as indeed for many theologians today), it is not so much the case that 'father' is a substitute or metaphor for 'God' as it is that 'father' and 'god' are both metaphoric and circumlocutory, expedients in the attempt to name the ineffable." See also Reinhartz, "'Father' as Metaphor," 6–7.

3. E.g., Exodus 15:3; while translations often have the gender-neutral *God is a warrior*, the Heb. syntax literally reads: *YHWH [is a] man of war* (cf. Isa 42:13). Contra Numbers 23:9a; 1 Samuel 15:29; Job 9:32; Hosea 11:9 where it states that God is not a man. See further Wijk-Bos, *Reimagining God*, 35–49.

4. Bennett, "Fatherhood of God," 12–23.

5. Filtvedt, "Father in the Gospel of John," 90–118; Widdicombe, "Father in the Gospel of John," 105–25. Cf. D'Angelo, "Intimating Deity," 59–82; Elshout, "Father and the Son in the Gospel of John," 41–55.

the writers of the epistles and apocalypse.[6] Subsequently, the Old and New Testaments are simultaneously viewed to draw out key themes of God, particularly the character traits of a father; this investigation determines what is revealed about God and hence how to relate to God. Finally, the generational function of fatherhood, both natural and spiritual, is briefly registered (to be more fully developed in chapter 6).

1.1 God as Father in the Old Testament

There are a couple times in the Old Testament where God as creator is explicitly conflated with God as father.[7] The prophet Malachi articulates, "'Have we not all one father? Has not one God created us?'" (Mal 2:10b, NRSV; cf. Mal 1:6). Likewise, Moses advances, "Is not he [i.e., God] your father, who created you, who made you and established you?" (Deut 32:6b, NRSV). The association of creator with father evokes the figurative properties of God's procreation.

In Deuteronomy 32:6b, the (Heb.) terms *created* (*qn'*), *made* (*'sh*), and *established* (*kûn*) may seem to evoke architectural or construction connotations; however, the imbedded imagery is that of birthing. This is corroborated with Job 31 where most of the same terminology (*made* [*'sh*] and *fashioned* [*kûn*]) occurs: "Did not he [God] who made me in the womb make them [i.e., his servants]? And did not one fashion us in the womb?" (Job 31:15, NRSV). The reference to *womb* in Job 31 naturally favors motherly imagery (see chapter 2, 2.1.2), so there are mixed metaphors throughout the Old Testament. Even within the same passage, though, the multivalence is exhibited; later in the Song of Moses (Deut 32:6b), God both sires (fatherly aspect) and births (motherly aspect) the children of Israel (Deut 32:18).

6. The word "father" is used 236 times in the New Testament, including sixty-three in Matthew, Mark, and Luke; ninety-three in John; and eighty in Acts–Revelation.

7. See Wright, *God the Father*; Soskice, *Kindness of God*, 66–83.

In the Psalter, God is hailed by the psalmists to be a father. The following stanzas attribute God's fatherly qualities as being provider and protection, security and salvation, and compassionate.

- Father of orphans and protector of widows is God in his holy habitation. (Ps 68:5, NRSV)
- "You are my Father, my God, and the Rock of my salvation!" (Ps 89:26, NRSV)
- As a father has compassion for his children, so the LORD has compassion for those who fear him. (Ps 103:13, NRSV)

God's parenthood of orphans is developed in chapter 5; alternatively, the compassion of God is the same characteristic prized of God as mother in Isaiah 49:15, which is taken up in chapter 2 (2.1.1).[8]

Isaiah and Jeremiah make mention of God in terms of father. Isaiah confesses, "you are our father . . . you, O LORD, are our father; our Redeemer" (Isa 63:16, NRSV); and "O LORD, you are our Father; we are the clay, and you are our potter; we are all the work of your hand" (Isa 64:8, NRSV; cf. Jer 18:1–11; Sir 33:10–13).[9] Additionally, the renowned prophecy of Isaiah 9:6 contains many monikers including that of father: "a child has been born for us, a son given to us . . . [who] is named Wonderful Counselor, Mighty God, Everlasting Father, Prince of Peace" (NRSV).[10]

Jeremiah, similarly, has the following statements rhetorically emanating from the mouth of God: "Have you not just now called to me, 'My Father, you are the friend of my youth'" (Jer 3:4, NRSV); and "I thought you would call me, My Father, and would not turn from following me" (Jer 3:19b, NRSV). Whereas the Isaianic references acclaim the character of *Father* God, the avowals in Jeremiah indicts the (collective) child (of Judah) of not being in the likeness of her Divine Parent (cf. 1.5).

8. Darr, *Isaiah's Vision*, 110.

9. See Niskanen, "Yhwh as Father, Redeemer, and Potter," 397–407.

10. Cf. Darr, *Isaiah's Vision*, 69–82.

In sum, there are only about a dozen references to God as father in the Old Testament. The word "Father," in these passages, is set either in apposition or in synonymous parallelism with God as creator, redeemer, protector, and ruler. Several metaphors and images are attributed to God, therefore, in order to display the fullness of the Deity.[11]

1.2 God as a Good, Gift-Giving Father

One primary attribute of God through the metaphorical lens of a father is that of a good, gift-giving parent. The benevolence of God is a familiar concept; yet, it is perhaps more poignant and personal when conceiving God as a good, gift-giving father. Both Jesus and James attest to this.

James writes, "Every good gift and every perfect gift is from above, coming down from the Father of lights with whom there is no variation or shadow due to change" (Jas 1:17, ESV). The maxim in this verse is that God is immutable, i.e., God does not change (v.17bβ). "God is said to be the 'Father of lights,' which is a creation metaphor."[12] As light from the sun generates and sustains life on earth (cf. Ps 104), so God is the source of all life (see further chapter 2). Life itself is a gift, and everything which makes life satisfying, enjoyable, and fulfilling are subsidiary gifts, or grace upon grace (John 1:16), from God.

James undoubtedly drew the tenet of God being a good, gift-giving father from Jesus. In Jesus' teaching on the mount/plain, he expounds upon this certitude.

11. Cf. Miller, *Biblical Faith and Fathering.*

12. Garland, "Severe Trials, Good Gifts, and Pure Religion," 392. Garland continues, explaining, "[God] created the stars (Gen. 1:14–18; Ps. 136:7; Jer. 4:23; 31:35; Sir. 43:1–12), and these created lights vary in their intensity and regularly wax and wane in the heavens. They can change from white dwarfs to red giants to black holes; God's goodness, however, is not as periodic as the full moon or the morning sunrise. It does not fade into the west" ("Severe Trials, Good Gifts, and Pure Religion," 392).

> Is there anyone among you who, if your child asks for a fish, will give a snake instead of a fish? Or if the child asks for an egg, will give a scorpion? If you then, who are evil, know how to give good gifts to your children, how much more will the heavenly Father give the Holy Spirit to those who ask him! (Luke 11:11–13, NRSV; cf. Matt 7:9–11)

This contrast is stark. If the good gift of a human is food, God's best gift is God's own self—the Holy Spirit. God's differential in goodness and generosity, consequently, is sacred and eternal.

In the so-called Lord's Prayer, too, God is described by Jesus as a father—even, *Our Father*—whose name, will, and kingdom are sacred and to be gloriously venerated (Matt 6:9b–10); additionally, God bestows upon the disciples of Jesus provision, pardon, and protection (Matt 6:11–13).[13] These are incredible gifts by which children of God may experience life on earth as it becomes saturated by heaven's reign. Children, incidentally, are the best at receiving gifts from their parents (cf. Matt 19:13–15; Mark 10:13–16; Luke 18:15–17).

1.3 God as a Loving and Just Father

God is also portrayed in the Bible as a father in terms of a parent who loves one's child and deals justly with children. There is no shortage of scriptural attestations which convey God's love for humanity, and specifically for God's (covenant) children. First John 3:1–2 (CEB) is a superlative example: "See what kind of love the Father has given to us in that we should be called God's children, and that is what we are! . . . Dear friends, now we are God's children . . ." Yet, the aspect of God's justice—or God's punishment—is sometimes misunderstood and problematic.

The Quran, for example, takes issue with (YHWH) God's loving nature together with God's judgment and punishment. Criticizing this as a logical contradiction, Sura 5:18 also equips the Islamic adherent with an apologetic: "The Jews and Christians

13. See Pennington, *Sermon on the Mount*, 220–24.

have said: 'We are Allah's [i.e., God's] children and His beloved.' Say: 'Why then does He punish you for your sins? You are rather human beings, part of those whom He has created. He forgives whom He pleases and punishes whom He pleases.'" However, the love of God and God's punishment are not mutually exclusive tenets; it is, rather, a paradox that can be resolved.

In Proverbs 1–9, the authorial persona is a wise father teaching and guiding his son. Once the narrator admonishes, "My child, do not despise the LORD's discipline or be weary of his reproof, for the LORD reproves the one he loves, as a father the son in whom he delights" (Prov 3:11–12, NRSV; cf. also Deut 8:5). The author of Hebrews too reconciles the paradox of God being both just and loving in the same manner, elaborating upon it further.

> Bear hardship for the sake of discipline. God is treating you like sons and daughters! What child isn't disciplined by his or her father? But if you don't experience discipline, which happens to all children, then you are illegitimate and not real sons and daughters. What's more, we had human parents who disciplined us, and we respected them for it. How much more should we submit to the Father of spirits and live? Our human parents disciplined us for a little while, as it seemed best to them, but God does it for our benefit so that we can share his holiness. No discipline is fun while it lasts, but it seems painful at the time. Later, however, it yields the peaceful fruit of righteousness for those who have been trained by it. (Heb 12:7–11, CEB)

Consequently, part of the way the vast extent of God's love is demonstrated to the children of God is precisely by lovingly correcting them.[14] Moreover, that God's justice is tempered with grace and mercy—and yet somehow still just(ice)—is a feat of divine economy and a mysterious, miraculous benefit unto humankind (see further in next sections).[15]

14. Goswell ("2 Samuel 7," 93) sagaciously illustrates how "the abject failure of Eli, Samuel, and David" (as well as other fathers) "to discipline their sons" serves as counter examples.

15. See further Keller, *Generous Justice*.

1.4 God as a Merciful Father

Arguably the most renowned and reputed attribute of God in the Bible is God's mercifulness. In the Old Testament, God self-identifies as "'The LORD, the LORD, a God merciful and gracious, slow to anger, and abounding in steadfast love and faithfulness'" (Exod 34:6, NRSV). This is God's acclaim throughout the Hebrew Bible (Deut 4:31; 2 Chr 30:9; Neh 9:17, 31; Pss 78:38; 86:15; 103:8; 111:4; 144:8; Joel 2:13; Jonah 4:2; Lam 4:10; cf. also Sir 2:11).[16] While the full complex of characteristics is enumerated in only about half the cited references, the attributes constant in the truncated refrains are the merciful and gracious quality of God.

Within the context of Jesus' teaching to love one's enemies, Jesus cites the famous character of God; Jesus proclaims: "'Be merciful, just as your Father is merciful'" (Luke 6:36, NRSV; cf. Matt 5:48). Whereas the Old Testament says *God* or *the LORD* in these stock phrases, Jesus echoes the merciful attribute of God while calling the LORD *Father*, and thereby modeling for his disciples to do the same. Consequently, it is the mercy or compassion (Gk. *oiktirmōn*) of (Father) God which reconciles the paradox of God's love (favor), on the one hand, and God's justice (punishment), on the other.[17] Jesus adjures his disciples, therefore, to be like, to act in the same manner as, their Father—namely, in being merciful and extending mercy (cf. Mic 6:8).

1.5 Fatherhood and Emulation

The notion of emulating one's father (denoted in Luke 6:36) is of paramount importance in Jewish culture; indeed, every child (son/daughter) was to emulate and, eventually and invariably, grow into

16. See further Comer, *God Has a Name*.

17. Relatedly, Besançon Spencer ("Father-Ruler," 440) observes: "Josephus refers to Zeus as 'nominally Father, but in reality a tyrant and a despot.' In contrast, the Biblical metaphor 'father' draws out a paradoxical picture of a very powerful father who is also very tender."

their parent (father/mother).[18] Similarly, the same is true on a divine scale, with God. Jesus saliently illustrates this in his Sermon on the Mount: "'But I say to you, love your enemies and pray for those who harass you so that you will be acting as children of your Father who is in heaven'" (Matt 5:44–45a, CEB; cf. Luke 6:35). Loving one's enemies is imitating the Divine Parent, because God extravagantly loves enemies of God unto reconciliation and salvation (John 3:16–17; Rom 5:5–9; Eph 2:4–8; 2 Cor 5:18–20; 1 John 4:9–10).

In John 8, Jesus elaborates upon the topic of fatherhood and emulation, juxtaposing different (metaphorical) fathers and the pursuit characteristics and deeds of their respective (metaphorical) children. The broader literary context presents the theme of the masses—particularly the Jews—trying to determine Jesus' origin and identity based on his teachings and actions. Correspondingly, Jesus also evaluates the parentage of the Jewish people, to whom he is speaking, determinant on their words and deeds.[19]

> Jesus replied, "If God were your Father, you would love me, for I came from God. Here I am. I haven't come on my own. God sent me. Why don't you understand what I'm saying? It's because you can't really hear my words. Your father is the devil. You are his children, and you want to do what your father wants. He was a murderer from the beginning. He has never stood for the truth, because there's no truth in him. Whenever that liar speaks, he speaks according to his own nature, because he's a liar and the father of liars. Because I speak the truth, you don't believe me. Who among you can show I'm guilty of sin? Since I speak the truth, why don't you believe me? God's children listen to God's words. You don't listen to me because you aren't God's children." (John 8:42–47, CEB)

Up to this point in the dialogue, Jesus has intimated his foregone conclusion. Previously the Jews had claimed, "Our father is

18. Wilkins, "Imitate, Imitators," 3:392. Cf. Michaelis, "μιμέομαι κλη," 4:659–74.

19. Cf. Howard-Brook, *Becoming Children of God*, 205–8.

Abraham" (John 8:39, CEB), and then "[t]he only Father we have is God!" (John 8:41, CEB). However, Jesus evaluates that based on their slavery to sin, their father is not righteous Abraham, and based on their inability to recognize and understand the Word of God (cf. John 1:1), Jesus draws a conclusion antithetical to his interlocutors. In short, Jesus' argument is: God speaks the language of truth, and God's legitimate children are fluent in that language; the devil speaks lies, and the devil's children are conversant in untruthfulness and falsehood.[20]

In this vantage, Jesus is not only declared to be God's son but also the exact representation of God. Jesus emulates his father with such adeptness that, by the end of the Gospel account, he has grown into and becomes his Father, so to speak. Like the criteria from the discourse in John 8, Jesus "say[s] just what the Father has taught [him]" to say (John 8:28, CEB); and "[w]hatever the Father does, the Son does likewise" (John 5:19, CEB). Therefore, in both articulation and action, Jesus is one with his Father (John 10:30) to the extent that "[w]hoever has seen me [i.e., Jesus] has seen the Father" (John 14:9, CEB).[21]

Furthermore, Jesus prays the same result for his disciples—that, by the Holy Spirit, they may be one with the Father just as the Son and the Father are one (John 17:11–23). The apostle Paul also desires disciples of Christ to ever grow in discipleship, i.e., Christlikeness; and this is expressed in familial terms. "Therefore be imitators of God, as beloved children, and live in love, as Christ loved us and gave himself up for us, a fragrant offering and sacrifice to God" (Eph 5:1–2, NRSV). Discipleship as children of God emulating their Divine Parent is a topic that will be returned to and developed later (see chapter 6).

To summarize, "God is Father not because God is masculine. God is Father because 'father' in the ancient world was a helpful metaphor to communicate certain aspects of God's character."[22]

20. Vellanickal, *Divine Sonship*, 252–63.

21. Cf. Reinhartz, "'Father' as Metaphor," 8.

22. Besançon Spencer, "Father-Ruler," 442.

Primarily, God's character includes being good, gracious, loving, just, and merciful. Concomitant to God's attributes, God's pursuant roles are creator and maker, redeemer and savior, provider and protector, and ruler and leader.

Anthropologically speaking, to be a father implies both children and procreative activity with a female. In the next chapter, God as metaphorically portrayed in the Bible as a mother is investigated. Subsequently, focus is given to God's child who is both metaphorically portrayed as a son (chapter 3) and as a daughter (chapter 4).

2

God as Mother

INVERSE TO THE PREVIOUS chapter, "God as Father," this chapter examines the canon of Scripture for how God is metaphorically portrayed as a mother; indeed, feminine verbiage used to depict God is implicitly inferred in the matter of the image of God (see the introduction).[1] This chapter, then, examines the maternal ways and motherly characteristics ascribed to each member of the Trinity. The First (God), Second (Messiah), and Third (Holy Spirit) Members of the Godhead alike are depicted in feminine terms.[2] Truly, an evident portrait emerges, as a mosaic, through the assemblage of biblical texts and imagery.

2.1 God (the First Person of the Godhead) as Mother

There are two primary ways in which the First Person of the Godhead is metaphorically portrayed as a mother in the Bible; first, how God is a comforter or womb-like, and second how God is a creator or birther. These aspects of God will be developed respectively. In addition, there are other feminine theriomorphisms (the ascription of animal characteristics) attributed to God which

1. See further Wijk-Bos, *Reimagining God*, 23–26; Stiebert, *Fathers and Daughters*, 176–85.

2. Cf. Soskice, *Kindness of God*, 100–124.

deserve mention, though these ancillary metaphoric images do not, on their own rite, comprise a robust motif.

2.1.1 Comforter/Womb-like

The feminine anthropomorphic aspect of God is most prominently and explicitly featured in the prophet Isaiah. Framed in divine speech, for instance, God says through the prophet, "As a mother comforts her child, so I will comfort you; in Jerusalem you will be comforted" (Isa 66:13, CEB). In this simile and through synonymous parallelism, God is like the mother; and it is with maternal comfort for a young child that God cares for the Israelite exiles. This message of comfort here near the end of Isaiah is an *inclusio*, a bookend, to the message of comfort that opens the second part of Isaiah:[3] "Comfort, comfort my people! says your God" (Isa 40:1, CEB). Thus, with comfort—as only a mother can give—does God comfort the remnant of the chosen people.

The mother metaphor of God is developed in more detail in Isaiah, specifically in terms of female anatomy. God says, "Listen to me, O house of Jacob, all the remnant of the house of Israel, who have been borne by me from your birth, carried from the womb; even to your old age I am he, even when you turn gray I will carry you. I have made, and I will bear; I will carry and will save" (Isa 46:3–4, NRSV). There is a paronomasia in the Hebrew language between the words "comfort" (*nḥm*) and "womb" (*rḥm*), inferring association; further, "womb" and "compassion" derive from the same cognate (Heb. *rḥm*).[4]

Therefore, for God to be compassionate (Ps 116:5b) is, in a sense, for God to be womb-like, and vise-versa. This ontology is also evident in the following Isaianic verse: "Can a woman forget her nursing child, or show no compassion [*rḥm*] for the child of her womb [*rḥm*]? Even these may forget, yet I will not forget you"

3. For the compositional nature of Isa 40–66, see e.g. Childs, *Isaiah*, 289–91, 440–49.

4. BDB 933; *HALOT* 2:1216–18.

(Isa 49:15, NRSV).[5] This rhetorical question underscores how unthinkable it is for God to neglect God's child(ren) by drawing upon probably the most powerful primal and protective illustration known to humans. Consequently, the child of God's womb (*rḥm*) will be showed compassion (*rḥm*) and comfort (*nḥm*)—for this is intrinsic to motherhood, to Godhood.

The implied imagery of breasts associated with God, in the verses mentioned here, are presumed elsewhere in Scripture, furthermore. In the Old Testament, one name of God is *El Shaddai* (e.g., Gen 17:1; Exod 6:3). Typically translated idiomatically as *God Almighty*,[6] Heb. *šadday* connotes mountains (via an Akkadian cognate);[7] alternatively, *shad* means (female) breast in Heb.,[8] and when inflected in the dual declension in conjunction with a divine moniker it renders something like *God of Breasts*.[9] The cognitive link between mountains and breasts (beyond lexemic considerations)—and the correlation of God as Almighty—is the following.[10] Like a mother's breastmilk provides total sustenance for the infant, so too God is the source of holistic provision for humans and animals; the image illustrating this is the rich nutrition from a mountain (e.g., Mount Zaphon), where the runoff of snow and rain descends its slopes fertilizing the land unto vegetation for food and sustained life. Such is the self-generative, self-sufficiency of God, and the dependency and need of people and fauna upon God (cf. Ps 104).

In the New Testament, also, the imagery of God's breasts is appropriated. The apostle Peter states: "Like newborn infants, long for the pure, spiritual milk, so that by it you may grow into

5. Cf. Løland, *Silent Or Salient Gender?*, 161–92; Dille, *Mixing Metaphors*, 128–51; Wijk-Bos, *Reimaging God*, 61–64.

6. Walker, "Divine Name Shaddai," 64–66.

7. BDB 994–95; *HALOT* 2:1420–22.

8. BDB 994; *HALOT* 2:1416–18. See e.g. Song of Songs 1:13; 4:5; 7:4, 8–9; 8:1, 8, 10.

9. "El Shaddai, literally means God with two breasts" (Ekblad, *Reading the Bible with the Damned*, 199). See also Albright, "Names SHADDAI and ABRAM," 180–93; Wijk-Bos, *Reimaging God*, 26–28.

10. All these key terms are exhibited in constellation in Genesis 49:25–26.

salvation—if indeed you have tasted that the Lord is good" (1 Pet 2:2–3, NRSV). Newborn infants naturally breastfeed, suckling from their mother; and, in salvation-life God is as the nursing mother to the spiritual baby (Ps 131:2).[11] This illustrative simile is the epistle writer's conceptual embellishment of a citation from Psalm 34:8a: "O taste and see that the LORD is good" (NRSV). Therefore, through an evocative metaphor, God's providence and provision is depicted in terms of a child being nourished and sustained by God for salvation-life as suckling, as feeding (cf. Heb 5:12–14), from her bosom.[12]

2.1.2 Creator/Birther

If God is womb-like (compassionate), then, after a gestational period, birthing is the natural result. God is often hailed as *Creator*; yet, some of the biblical language for the act of creation is God *birthing* things, and even people, into existence (Deut 32:18; Isa 46:3–4; cf. also Num 11:11–12).[13] This birthing terminology is rendered in the poetic portions of the Bible.

In the book of Job, after the long deliberation between Job and his friends (Job 3–31), God speaks. Part of the divine speech, which God delivers from the tempest, conveys the majesty of the creation acts performed by God and its subsidiary intricacies preserved by the providence of God. In rhetoric redolent of majestic supremacy, God at one point asks Job:

> Where were you when I laid the earth's foundations?
> . . . Who set its measurements?

11. See Mollenkott, *Divine Feminine*, 20–25.

12. A related phenomenon exists in Egyptology. "Hathor . . . was notable for her role as divine wet nurse. In the Middle Kingdom, King Nebhepetre Mentuhotep had himself portrayed in his funerary chapel at Dendera as suckling from the breast of Hathor, the goddess who, in bovine form, also nursed the child god Horus . . ." (Budin, "Reduced to Her Bare Essentials," 170). See also the statuettes of goddess Isis suckling infant god Horus.

13. Cf. Løland, *Silent Or Salient Gender?*, 129–60; Darr, *Isaiah's Vision*, 105–9 (205–24); Crouch, "Humanity's Divine Parentage," 12–15.

> . . . On what were its footings sunk; who laid its cornerstone,
> . . . Who enclosed the Sea behind doors when it burst forth from the womb . . .
> (Job 38:4–8, CEB; cf. Ps 90:2; Isa 42:14–15)[14]

Indirectly, the sea sources from God's womb. Could the sea be figuratively equivalent to amniotic fluids in the birthing of the world? Indeed, the poetry evokes how like after a pregnant woman's water breaks (i.e., the rupturing of the amniotic sac) there is shortly thereafter the advent of life!

Similar imagery is utilized in the creation account of Genesis 1 when referring to the same creative acts of God. The opening verses of the Bible read, "In the beginning, God created the heavens and the earth. The earth was without form and void, and darkness was over the face of the deep. And the Spirit of God was hovering over the face of the waters" (Gen 1:1–2, ESV). The Spirit of God's "hovering" (Heb. *mrḥpt*), grammatically speaking, is a participle of feminine declension; and the imagery of the verb connotes a (female) bird-like action. Thus, Genesis 1 may, like Job 38, poetically convey a female figure who—when her water breaks—issues forth life, creation.[15]

2.1.3 Ancillary Theriomorphic Maternal References

In addition to the feminine bird-like reference of God's Spirit hovering over the watery mass of pre-creation, there is another bird analogy made of God in the Pentateuch with the same hovering action (Heb. *rḥp*). In his song, Moses depicts God in the following way: "As an eagle stirs up its nest, and hovers over its young; as it spreads its wings, takes them up, and bears them aloft on its pinions" (Deut 32:11, NRSV; cf. Exod 19:4).[16] It is the wings,

14. Cf. Løland, *Silent Or Salient Gender?*, 100–128; Dille, *Mixing Metaphors*, 41–73; Wijk-Bos, *Reimaging God*, 51–55, 58–59.

15. Wijk-Bos, *Reimaging God*, 72–74.

16. While the grammar is inflected in the masculine throughout this verse, it is the mother who tends to the young as so described. Tigay (*Deuteronomy*, 304) notes that to "rouse," or "stir up" (NRSV), is from Heb. "*ya'ir* [which]

particularly, which provides motherly protection.[17] This maternal protecting sentiment also finds similar animalistic analogy in Hosea; there, God says, "I will fall upon them like a bear robbed of her cubs, and will tear open the covering of their heart; there I will devour them like a lion, as a wild animal would mangle them" (Hos 13:8, NRSV).[18] What is underscored in the foregoing verses is the caring role that God as mother plays.[19]

2.2 Messiah (the Second Person of the Godhead) as Mother

Though the Messiah/Christ of God incarnates in a male body, at times the biblical literature is suggestive of Jesus embodying typically maternal instincts and exclusively maternal roles. The feminine/motherly attributes of Jesus the Messiah/Christ, as stylistically rendered in the Gospels, is most acutely evident in his passion, specifically, and the last week of his life, generally.

2.2.1 Comforter/Compassionate

At the beginning of passion week, Jesus' inclination to comfort the children of Israel is accentuated. Just as God is theriomorphically

---

may mean 'protects'" (term originally in bold typeface). Cf. Mollenkott, *Divine Feminine*, 83–91.

17. God's wings feature most predominately in the Psalter (Pss 17:8; 36:7; 57:1; 61:4; 63:7; 91:4). Though still a theriomorphism, God's wings are often likened to a refuge (tower) in which the psalmist takes shelter. Interestingly, Ps 63:7 reads, "in the shadow of your wings I sing for joy" (NRSV), making the psalmist's song equivalent to that of a hatchling's chirping within God's nurturing embrace. See further, Gillmayr-Bucher, "Body Images in the Psalms," 301–26.

18. Mays, *Hosea*, 175: "A she-bear robbed of her cubs was a particularly vivid imagery of fury (Prov. 17.12; II Sam. 17.8)" (Mays, *Hosea*, 176). Garrett, *Hosea, Joel*, 259: "Yahweh has been robbed of his children (the common people of Israel) by his wife (the woman Israel, that is, the royal and priestly leadership). She has made them to be the children of Baal."

19. Wijk-Bos, *Reimaging God*, 66–72; Mollenkott, *Divine Feminine*, 49–53.

an eagle via simile (Deut 32:11) and like a nondescript bird (Gen 1:2), Jesus likens himself to a female bird as he laments Jerusalem's fate. Entering the holy city for a religious festival (Passover), Jesus bemoans: "'Jerusalem, Jerusalem! You who kill the prophets and stone those who were sent to you. How often I wanted to gather your people together, just as a hen gathers her chicks under her wings. But you didn't want that'" (Matt 23:37, CEB).[20]

Incredibly tenderly, Jesus desires to tuck in his little chicks (i.e., the people of God) for protection and in love.[21] The Second Person of the Godhead is like the First when metaphorically self-identifying as a comforting mother-like figure (see Isa 66:13). Similarly, Jesus is often animated by compassion (that womb-like quality) when he interacts with people.[22] To take one example, compassion causes Jesus to propel his disciples into the liberation mission in which he is already engaged.

> Now when Jesus saw the crowds, he had compassion for them because they were troubled and helpless, like sheep without a shepherd. Then he said to his disciples, 'The size of the harvest is bigger than you can imagine, but there are few workers. Therefore, plead with the Lord of the harvest to send out workers for his harvest.' (Matt 9:36–38, CEB; cf. Luke 15:20).

Thus, Jesus' propensity for compassion and comfort, which is typically reserved for mothers of her child(ren), is his impulse for the children of Israel, and especially his disciples and future disciples.

20. Even the nomenclature *passion week* parallels *compassion*; for, *compassion* mean to suffer (*passion*) with (*com-*) someone, and so Jesus does with and on the behalf of humanity.

21. See Mollenkott, *Divine Feminine*, 92–96; cf. also Mollenkott, *Divine Feminine*, 44–48.

22. See Matthew 9:36/14:14 and Mark 6:34; Matthew 15:32 and Mark 8:2; Matthew 20:34; Luke 7:13; 15:20.

2.2.2 Birther/Creator

Unique to motherhood is the capacity to give birth; and this too finds counterpart in the life of Jesus. As the Old Testament poetically purports God's creation as a birthing, a loose association of the same with Jesus is present in the New Testament. Though Jesus is a male,[23] his last act on the cross is reminiscent of a woman giving birth.[24]

At the end of passion week, upon Jesus dying on the cross, "one of the soldiers pierced his side with a spear, and immediately blood and water came out" (John 19:34, CEB). It has been proposed that the issuing of blood and water evokes birthing, namely amniotic fluids; and, therefore, what Jesus births is the church.[25] Indeed, like a woman who dies in delivery while the child is spared and lives, so Jesus gives his life up to give birth, give life to his children; and Jesus' children, as it were, are defined in the New Testament as the church (cf. Matt 16:18), the faithful of the kingdom of God whose adherence and loyalty is to Jesus the Christ (cf. John 18:28–40).[26]

This interpretation may seem like symbolism stretched too far; however, this reading is substantiated when corroborating Psalm 22. Psalm 22 is that lament Jesus cites when on the cross; he, in articulating the words of the psalmist, decries, "My God, my God, why have you forsaken me?" (Ps 22:1, NRSV). Within the same psalm there are specific references that all have striking resonance with and fulfillment in Jesus' crucifixion; these include [1] the protagonist receiving verbatim words of mocking (Ps 22:8; Matt 27:43), [2] being pierced in the hands and feet by encircled enemies (Ps 22:16; Matt 27:35a; Mark 15:24a; Luke 23:33; John 19:23a), and [3] having his garment divided and casting lots for

23. For reasons to be explained in chapter 5.

24. See Soskice, *Kindness of God*, 86–91.

25. See Levine, *Feminist Companion to John*, 205n73.

26. Of course, at the resurrection the image changes: Jesus is a living "mother" who enjoys life with the children of God.

his cloak (Ps 22:18; Matt 27:35b; Mark 15:24b; Luke 23:34b; John 19:23b–24).

In addition, there are also a couple stanzas in Psalm 22 which depict God as a midwife and the psalmist as a newborn child (cf. also Isa 66:6–9).[27] The psalmist prays to God the following: "Yet it was you who took me from the womb; you kept me safe on my mother's breast. On you I was cast from my birth, and since my mother bore me you have been my God" (Ps 22:9–10, NRSV).[28] If Jesus is the Messiah that fulfills all prophecy, including the semi-prophetic psalms,[29] then the cited verses characterize Jesus' salvific act on the cross.

In anticipation of his redemptive work on the cross, Jesus portrays its process and agony as well as its rejoicing and happiness in part of his Farewell Discourse in the Gospel of John.[30] Jesus does so by utilizing a birthing analogy, which he himself is to undertake and experience.

> When a woman is in labor, she has pain, because her hour has come. But when her child is born, she no longer remembers the anguish because of the joy of having brought a human being into the world. So you have pain now; but I will see you again, and your hearts will rejoice, and no one will take your joy from you. (John 16:21–22, NRSV)

Jesus' comparative illustration of child-birthing to describe his crucifixion and subsequent resurrection is poignant. Indeed, "Jesus . . . endured the cross . . . for the sake of the joy that was laid out in front of him, and sat down at the right side of God's throne" (Heb 12:2, CEB). Jesus' *birthing* of the church (i.e., those redeemed

27. So Trible, "Depatriarchalizing," 33; McGregor Wright, "God, Metaphor and Gender," 296; Mollenkott, *Divine Feminine*, 32–35.

28. The imagery of the psalmist being placed (cast) upon God at birth is reminiscent of the child-birthing practice of immediately placing the newborn upon the mother's bosom for skin-to-skin, bonding time.

29. Cf. Gunkel and Begrich, *Psalms*, 251.

30. See Watt, *Family of the King*, 109–10. Cf. also Feuillet, "L'heure de la femme," 169–84; 361–80; 557–73.

by regeneration) was worth the pain of delivery, notwithstanding any postpartum blues (i.e., Jesus' ascending and being enthroned on high).

2.2.3 (Re)born of God

The epistle of 1 John is the only place in the Bible where the phrase "born of God" occurs, and there seven times; for example, "Everyone who believes that Jesus is the Christ has been born of God" (1 John 5:1a NRSV; cf. 1 John 3:9 [2x]; 4:7; 5:4, 18 [2x]). The act of God birthing naturally evokes motherly connotations, as it is a female capacity. This phrase "born of God" indicates that the Johannine community (i.e., John's disciples in Christ) understood Jesus' work on the cross as the means by which one may undergo salvific regeneration—just as the Gospel of John evidences (see again John 16:21–22; 19:34). Being born of God or born again was, of course, that vital topic of conversation which Jesus had with Nicodemus (John 3:1–8; cf. 1:12–13).[31]

In his epistle, Paul, similarly, perhaps harkens back to the creation account of Genesis 1 when speaking of the regeneration of Jesus-disciples as a new creation, a new creature. "So if anyone is in Christ, there is a new creation: everything old has passed away; see, everything has become new!" (2 Cor 5:17, NRSV). It is fitting, therefore, that one sacrament of Christianity to signify regeneration or new birth is baptism—being immersed into waters and emerging from amniotic-like fluids into Christ indeed symbolizes becoming a new child of God (cf. Rom 6:3–11).

31. Watt, *Family of the King*, 170–88; Howard-Brook, *Becoming Children of God*, 86–89.

2.3 Holy Spirit (the Third Person of the Godhead) as Mother

The Holy Spirit, the Third Person of the Godhead, may also be perceived as a divine motherly figure;[32] in fact, it is often posited that the Holy Spirit is the most femininely portrayed and so understood in Scripture.[33] The Spirit of God has previously been mentioned when examining the hovering, bird-like activity at the start of creation (2.1.2) as well as the Holy Spirit playing a vital role in regeneration (2.2.3). Due to the triune (tri-unity) nature of God, it is indeed difficult to speak of one member of the Godhead without referring to the others. With this in consideration, the primary ways the Holy Spirit is depicted in feminine/motherly terms are those previously identified—namely, as creator/birther and comforter.

2.3.1 Creator/Birther

In Proverbs, wisdom is personified as a woman (Prov 1–9, 31);[34] moreover, Lady Wisdom is purported to have been complicit in the creation of the cosmos at the beginning (Prov 3:19–20; cf. Col 1:15–17). This figure is tantamount to God's own self, due to the acts of creation which are attributed to Wisdom.[35] There is, further, a reminiscent poetic equivalent between the (Holy) Spirit of God in Genesis 1:2 and Wisdom in Proverbs 3:19–20 (CEB)—"The

32. McGregor Wright notes: "In the Greek New Testament the word for Spirit (*pneuma*) is neuter, whereas in the Hebrew Old Testament the word for Spirit (*ruah*) is feminine" ("God, Metaphor and Gender," 288).

33. In other religions (particularly Greek mythology), there are whole family units within the pantheon of gods and goddesses. It is sometimes proposed, accordingly, that God is father and the Holy Spirit is mother who together conceive the son of God.

34. *Wisdom* is, in Heb., feminine declension (*HALOT* 1:314). That God is also like a woman in the sense that she is a mistress of the home, see Psalm 123:2 and Luke 15:8–10.

35. See Wijk-Bos, *Reimaging God*, 78–88; Stiebert, *Fathers and Daughters*, 185–88; Mollenkott, *Divine Feminine*, 97–105.

LORD laid the foundations of the earth with wisdom, establishing the heavens with understanding. With his knowledge, the watery depths burst open, and the skies drop dew"—such that the two may be understood as one and the same.

The Holy Spirit, further, is intimately involved in the conception of the Messiah, the creative act of incarnating an eternal being into human form. "The angel said to [Mary], 'The Holy Spirit will come upon you, and the power of the Most High will overshadow you; therefore the child to be born will be holy; he will be called Son of God'" (Luke 1:35, NRSV).[36] Likewise, the Holy Spirit generates new life for the one who believes in Jesus the Messiah (cf. John 3:5–7).

Indeed, though it is Jesus who gives a salvific invitation for eternal life, it is the Spirit of the Living God who mediates and actualizes that eternal living. This delineation is present in the following pronouncement of Jesus.

> . . . Jesus . . . cried out, 'Let anyone who is thirsty come to me, and let the one who believes in me drink. As the scripture has said, "Out of the believer's heart shall flow rivers of living water."' Now he said this about the Spirit, which believers in him were to receive; for as yet there was no Spirit, because Jesus was not yet glorified. (John 7:37–39, NRSV)

The author underscores the Holy Spirit's role in regeneration with the editorial note at the beginning of v.39 ("Now he said this about the Spirit"). A similar truth-claim and reality-invitation was offered by Jesus to the Samaritan woman at the well (John 4:10–11; cf. Jer 2:13; 17:13). It should be noted (again) that water issuing from or within a person evokes amniotic fluids; consequently, the Holy Spirit is conceptually analogous to the believer's never-ending life source (cf. Titus 3:4–6).

36. John the Baptizer, too, is "filled with the Holy Spirit even before his birth" (Luke 1:15, CEB); and his mother "Elizabeth was filled with the Holy Spirit" when "the child leaped in her womb" at "Elizabeth hear[ing] Mary's greeting" (Luke 1:41, CEB). Cf. Mollenkott, *Divine Feminine*, 15–19.

To be imbued with the Holy Spirit, or figurative steams of living water, is to enjoy salvation-relationship with the Triune, Living God. Spirit-filled new creations in Christ (2 Cor 5:17), furthermore, are all—irrespective of gender (identity)—participants, in a sense, in and like unto God as a mother; that is, all who are indwelled by the Holy Spirit are, as it were, carrying the Spirit like in pregnancy! Just as Mary was pregnant with the Son of God, so Jesus-disciples are pregnant with the Holy Spirit—a divine personage resides in both. So, just as Mary birthed Jesus, Spirit-filled Christians birth (or produce) the fruit of the Spirit (Gal 5:21–22) specifically and the life of Christ generally (Col 3:1–17). Like pregnancy, additionally, there is a gestational aspect of the resident Holy Spirit, insofar as sanctification is the process a Jesus-disciple being made holy (cf. 1 Thess 4:3–8; 5:23).

2.3.2 Comforter

As the First and Second Members of the Godhead are portrayed with the typical motherly aspect of comforter (2.1.1; 2.2.1), so too is the Third Member of the Godhead. Jesus once called the one whom he will send after his departure (death) the Comforter: "But the Comforter, which is the Holy Ghost, whom the Father will send in my name, he shall teach you all things, and bring all things to your remembrance, whatsoever I have said unto you" (John 14:26, KJV).[37]

Comfort in association with and a work of the Holy Spirit is mentioned a few times in the New Testament—chiefly, in conjunction with the life and ministry of the church. For example, Acts 9:31 (NRSV) states: "Meanwhile the church throughout Judea, Galilee, and Samaria had peace and was built up. Living in the fear of the Lord and in the comfort of the Holy Spirit, it increased in

37. Actually, only the KJV translates this nomenclature *comforter*; normally, the (Gk.) pronoun *paraclētos* is defined as *Helper, Intercessor, Mediator* (BDAG, 766). The notion of *comfort* comes from the (Gk.) noun *paraclēsis*, meaning *comfort, encouragement, consolation* (BDAG, 766); and the (Gk.) verb *parakaleō, to exhort, encourage, comfort* (BDAG, 764–65).

numbers" (cf. Luke 2:25; 1 Cor 14:3; Phil 2:1). Furthermore, the comfort of God is a leitmotif in 2 Corinthians 1:3–11, where (the Spirit of) God being the source of comfort is mentioned sevenscore—the highest concentration of *comfort* in any passage of the Bible (cf. 2 Thess 2:16).

In summary, each person of the Triune God metaphorically resembles a mother. Motherhood is primarily depicted of God in terms of birthing (creating) and being comforting or womb-like. The symbolism of water, in connection with creation, buttresses the birthing connotations as it evokes amniotic fluid; God's comforting and compassionate nature is also closely related to maternal protection and care, nurturing and rearing. Those who are born of (the Spirit of) God as mother are the church, children of God, regenerate disciples of Christ. Therefore, the (reborn) children of God participate in—by the grace of God—the same creative, generative, and transformative capacities, namely life in Christ and Christlikeness.

To be a parent, i.e., for God to be a father/mother, necessitates the existence of offspring, which is the subject of the next two chapters. Israel is at times presented as a firstborn son (chapter 3) and at other times as a foundling daughter (chapter 4). Furthermore, God as Divine Parent also adopts children into the family of God (chapter 5).

3

God as Parent of a Son

In this chapter, the personification of the Israelites as God's son will be surveyed throughout the Old Testament; the metaphor of Israel as son is rich and reasonably well-developed. The next chapter will examine the same subject, namely Israel as the progeny of God, yet in terms of how God's covenant people is portrayed as a female/daughter. The son Israel metaphor is addressed first (over against daughter Israel) simply because it is a concept developed earlier in the Bible (Pentateuch vs. Prophets, respectively).

Initially Israel's infancy is evoked in Exodus, and subsequently the toddler and adolescent stages are expounded by Hosea in referring to the wilderness wandering years and beyond; Jeremiah too portrays the Southern Kingdom as God's firstborn son. Alternatively, the Davidic king who sits on the throne in Jerusalem is the representative son of God on behalf of the populace. Coming to the New Testament, God's (only begotten) Son, Jesus of Nazareth, is revealed in the Gospels as sourcing from the Israelites, and is, furthermore, depicted as True Israel personified and the ultimate son of David, i.e. the Messiah. Throughout the Bible, the role of (divine) sonship is advanced and is therefore thematically examined herein.

3.1 Israel as God's Firstborn Son

3.1.1 Exodus 4–13

The Bible first conveys personified Israel as God's son in Exodus 4. After God reveals Godself to Moses in the burning bush and commissions him to serve as the human liberating agent for what would become the exodus of the Israelites from their generational slavery in Egypt, Moses is given a specific message from God to deliver to the pharaoh. Once Moses confronts Pharaoh, the former is to say to the latter, "Thus says the LORD: Israel is my firstborn son. I said to you, 'Let my son go that he may worship me.' But you refused to let him go; now I will kill your firstborn son" (Exod 4:22–23, NRSV).

This imperative is pronounced before the first confrontation between Moses and Pharaoh and before the advent of the ten plagues; yet, it foreshadows (as if already-completed time) the death of Pharaoh's firstborn concomitant of the tenth plague. In God's final plague upon Egypt, whereas the firstborn from the lowest of society to the highest in Egyptian society—and everyone in between—dies in one night (Exod 11:4–5; 12:29–30), the Israelites' firstborns are spared from the angel of death. God provided the redemptive solution of substitutionary sacrifice for the Hebrew people, but Pharaoh and the Egyptians were not privy to this salvation (Exod 11:1—12:28).

Whether or not the reference to Pharaoh's firstborn in Exodus 4:23 is a collective personification of all Egypt's firstborns (i.e., Pharaoh as the father of the nation) or a literal one (i.e., Pharaoh's own biological son) is somewhat ambiguous. On this note, Brevard Childs underscores the issue of sons and parentage; he explicates,

> That Israel is Yahweh's first-born son is a metaphor . . . but then the threat moves immediately beyond the metaphor to speak in grim, realistic terms of Pharaoh's first-born. Of course, when reading from the perspective of the subsequent events, one tends to overlook the enormous leap in associating two totally different concepts. But far more is at stake than an artistic literary device. The conflict is

> over parental power, and in the claim of the first-born the God of Israel and the king of Egypt have clashed in a head-on encounter.[1]

This is keen analysis. Alternatively, the wordplays in the Heb. text throughout Exodus 5–6 also juxtapose the competing claim of who is the rightful master of the Israelites:[2] are the Hebrews (העברים) God's servants/worshipers (עבדי),[3] or are the Hebrews (העברים) Pharaoh's slaves (מעבדים)?[4] Regardless of the imagery or metaphor, there is indeed a dueling between God and Pharaoh over the ownership of, or sovereignty over, the Israelites; and sonship of (YHWH) God contains much more dignity, value, and purpose than does being slaves of Pharaoh.

There is something paradigmatic, furthermore, about the literal firstborn sons of the Hebrew people as it relates to the metaphorical claim of God's parenthood of the Israelites. Within the narrative of the tenth plague, a legislative excursus ensues establishing an etiological tradition concerning every firstborn of all the tribes of Israel. Exodus 13, the first of many similar such passages in the Pentateuch, instructs Israel how (in perpetuity?) to redeem firstborn males; and this figurative ceremony serves to remind and inculcate the Israelites regarding Passover (Exod 12–13)—how the Hebrew firstborns had death *pass* them *over* because God provided means of redemption for them.

The Passover redemption dictum for the firstborn sons of Israel of Exodus 13 reads as follows.

> The LORD said to Moses: Dedicate to me all your oldest children. Each first offspring from any Israelite womb belongs to me, whether human or animal. Moses said to the people . . . you should set aside for the LORD whatever comes out of the womb first. All of the first males born

1. Childs, *Exodus*, 102.

2. Even without knowledge of the Hebrew language, one can see the orthographical similarities in the parenthetical words; and this is part-and-parcel of the paronomasia.

3. See Exodus 3:18; 5:3; 7:16; 9:1, 13; 10:3. Cf. Exodus 4:30–31; 6:7.

4. See Exodus 5:6, 10, 13–14. Cf. Exodus 5:15–16.

> to your animal belong to the LORD. But every first male donkey you should ransom with a sheep. If you don't ransom it, you must break its neck. You should ransom every oldest male among your children. When in the future your child asks you, 'What does this mean?' you should answer, 'The LORD brought us with great power out of Egypt, out of the place we were slaves. When Pharaoh refused to let us go, the LORD killed all the oldest offspring in the land of Egypt, from the oldest sons to the oldest male animals. That is why I offer to the LORD as a sacrifice every male that first comes out of the womb. But I ransom my oldest sons.' (Exod 13:1–3a, 12–15, CEB; cf. Exod 22:29b; 34:19–20; Num 8:17–18; 18:15–17)[5]

Therefore, since God saved the lives of the Israelite firstborns in Egypt, both those and all future firstborns[6]—viz., everyone in the community—are to be aware of and grateful for God's gift of (salvation) life.[7] Thus, even within the overarching metaphor of collective Israel being personified as God's firstborn son (Exod 4:22), there are literal and figurative, legislative and festive reverberations of the life and religion of Israel which illustrates an analogous equivalent (Exod 12–13).[8]

5. Stuart (*Exodus*, 729) interprets, "all firstborn humans must be redeemed [i.e. monetary payment] so that they could remain alive and with their families, even though from a theoretical point of view they would be Yahweh's property from birth."

6. Later, God separates one tribe (Levi) from the twelve tribes of Israel to minister as priests unto God and on behalf of the nation (see e.g. Num 3); while this is somewhat analogous to the stated practice, it is distinct.

7. Stuart (*Exodus*, 317), projecting into the New Testament, states: "The ultimate purpose of this instruction was to prepare the Israelites for the death of Christ on their behalf. . . . Paul's assertion in 1 Cor 6:20 and 7:23, 'You were bought with a price,' follows the logic of the Old Testament redemption system as it foreshadows the redemption price paid by Christ with his own blood."

8. Cf. Miller, *Biblical Faith and Fathering*, 71–79.

3.1.2 Exodus 2, 14–15

Whereas the implication of the statement in Exodus 4:22 is that personified Israel is already born, there is another sense in the narrative of Exodus 1–15 that the nation of Israel is birthed upon the event of the sea crossing (Exod 14).[9] A foreshadow of Israel's liberation and birthing can be seen in Moses' deliverance from the basket and adoption by Pharaoh's daughter; for, just as the infant Moses was drawn out of the waters—as amniotic fluids (cf. chapter 2)—by the Egyptian princess (Exod 2:10), so God would draw out the Israelites from Egypt via the Re(e)d Sea (Exod 14).[10] Further, that Miriam both aids in the first rescue (Exod 2:4–7) and facilitates worship at the subsequent salvation (Exod 15:20–21) links together these water rescue events, inviting parallelism. Consequently, the waters of Exodus 2 and 14–15 along with its connotations evokes the birthing of, or entering new life as, God's delivered firstborn son.

3.2 Israel in Toddler Stage and throughout the Rebellious Years

The metaphor of Israel as God's son is latter advanced by the prophets, namely Hosea and Jeremiah. In their prophetic material, the metaphor is expanded according to stages of childhood development and the character traits that are indicative of those stages. Thus, by spanning the stages of toddler, adolescent, and adult, the prophetic tradition recasts and (divinely) commentates on Israel's history with YHWH God. Yet before launching into that, one caveat must be mentioned.

In the law of the LORD, a rebellious son is prohibited; should the wayward son not heed his parents warning and persist in

9. Römer ("Exodus Narrative," 168) evinces: "The splitting of the sea in Exodus 14 is an act of creation, as is the separation of the waters in Genesis 1. In this text, God creates the world, while in Exodus 14 Yhwh creates Israel as his people by making them cross the waters."

10. Cf. Claassens, *Mourner, Mother, Midwife*, 69–71.

rebellion, then he would be liable to capital punishment (Deut 21:18–21). Thus, when the prophets decry Israel's sin of rebellion the charge and consequence is serious, indeed. Moreover, the communal rebellion of collective Israel (metaphorically God's son) denotes disobedience to the Sinaitic Covenant, Israel's law code, which is God's standard for obedience. When God—the metaphoric parent—chastens Israel, then, it is to correct God's son unto life and flourishing (cf. Deut 30:19–20).

3.2.1 Hosea 11

Hosea was one of the Hebrews' earliest prophets; he prophesied in eighth century BCE, and his audience was the northern kingdom of Israel. The historical backdrop against which Hosea finds himself is near the end of the Northern Kingdom's existence; the Assyrian Empire has been steadily oppressing Israel, and there are just a few more monarchs and decades before Israel will collapse completely and its peoples exiled. This nation's demise, the prophet maintains, has entirely to do with Israel's covenant unfaithfulness to YHWH God; and this becomes metaphorized as spiritual adultery—a graphic and consistent theme throughout Hosea.

Near the end of the book, though, Hosea utilizes another metaphor: personified Israel. Israel's history since the exodus is portrayed in a lifespan that ranges from infancy, to a toddler and adolescent, to a rebellious adult. In Hosea 11, the prophetic oracle is rendered thus.

> When Israel was a child, I loved him, and out of Egypt I called my son. The more I called them, the further they went from me; they kept sacrificing to the Baals, and they burned incense to idols. Yet it was I who taught Ephraim to walk; I took them up in my arms, but they did not know that I healed them. I led them with bands of human kindness, with cords of love. I treated them like those who lift infants to their cheeks; I bent down to them and fed them. . . . How can I give you up, Ephraim? How can I hand you over, Israel? . . . My heart winces within me; my

> compassion grows warm and tender. I won't act on the heat of my anger; I won't return to destroy Ephraim; for I am God and not a human being, the holy one in your midst; I won't come in harsh judgment. They will walk after the LORD, who roars like a lion. . . . and I will return them to their homes, says the LORD. (Hos 11:1–4, 8–11 CEB; cf. Deut 32:9–18)

There are some tremendously tender gestures in this passage which depict God's care and child-rearing of Israel as an infant and toddler. *I bent down to them and fed them* perhaps evokes a parent spoon-feeding an infant solid (really, puréed) foods in his highchair. *I treated them like those who lift infants to their cheeks* is a loving embrace which focuses on a baby's chubby checks upon a parent's own face and lips. *I led them with bands of human kindness, with cords of love* is suggestive of the infant who, reaching high to grips his parent's index fingers, is pulled and balanced along by the parent in guiding assisted steps; eventually the toddler does learn to walk unassisted—*it was I who taught Ephraim to walk*—and God as parent even scoops Israel up when he takes a tumble and scrapes his knee in order to cure the wound (*I took them up in my arms . . . I healed them*). These actions are indeed those of a nurturing, loving parent.

As Israel grows into adolescence and adulthood, however, the relationship between Divine Parent and son becomes strained and even tragic. Israel becomes obstinate and rebellious (*The more I called them, the further they went from me*), loyal to another god/parent over against YHWH (*they kept sacrificing to the Baals, and they burned incense to idols*), and fails to recognize the goodness of God (*but they did not know that I healed them*). God's reaction to such insolent defiance is remarkably sterling—precisely because, as God says, *I am God and not a human being, the holy one in your midst*. While God does punish God's rebellious son, Israel's punishment—namely, exile (vv. 5–6, 9–10)—is curtailed because of God's great love (vv. 1a, 4a) and compassion (v. 8c)!

This metaphorical paternal illustration thus vividly depicts God as a parent of a son, with all the joys and heartaches that accompany parenthood.

3.2.2 Numbers (in retrospect)

While the prophetic allegory of Hosea 11 summarizes Exodus through 1 Kings (and forecasts the exile detailed in 2 Kings 17), the toddler and adolescent stages appear to be specifically referring to young Israel in the wilderness wandering as encapsulated in Numbers. Indeed, (re)reading Numbers through the metaphorical lens of God as parent and Israel as child yields relevant interpretation (see Num 11:11–15).[11] A brief survey of events so rhetorically viewed depict Israel as a stubborn and rebellious son and God as a disciplinarian parent—who punishes in many creative and quite extreme ways.

God punished the Israelites by immolating people with fire (Num 11:1; 16:35); by causing the Israelites to wander in the desert unto death (Num 14 [32–34]); by unspecified plagues (Num 11:33; 16:46–50); by the Israelites losing battles (Num 14:39–45); by causing the earth to swallow up families alive (Num 16:25–34). Similarly, when the Israelites rebelled against God's appointed leaders—even when the leadership itself rebelled—extreme and creative punishments were also inflicted; these include (in addition to the cited methods) being plagued by leprosy (Num 12) and dying prematurely (Num 20:22–29; cf. Deut 34).

God also relents in punishment and restores the children of Israel. For example, God listens to intercessory prayer and intervenes (Num 11:2; 14:13–19; 21:7); God directs Aaron to perform an atonement rite which wards off a plague (Num 16:46–50); God grants military success against adversaries (Num 21:1–3, 21–35); God gives antidote for venomous snake bites (Num 21:8–9). Further, God reaffirms human leadership by advocating for Moses

11. Cf. Sakenfeld, "Divine Forgiveness," 327.

(Num 12:5–9) and reappointing Aaron by causing his staff to bud, blossom, and bare almonds (Num 17).

Consequently, whenever the Israelites grumbled against God or God's plan,[12] YHWH God became angry.[13] In meting out judgment upon God's stubborn and rebellious child, a parental discipline is imaged (cf. chapter 1); "for the LORD reproves the one he loves, as a father the son in whom he delights" (Prov 3:12, NRSV). In that vein, Moses commentates in hindsight that "'in the wilderness . . . the LORD your God bore you, as a man bears his son, in all the way that you went until you came to this place'" (Deut 1:31, RSV)—again illustrating the father–son metaphor.

3.2.3 Jeremiah

As with Hosea, God correspondingly speaks through the prophet Jeremiah proclaiming that Ephraim, an alternate name for the northern kingdom of Israel, is God's firstborn son (Jer 31:9, 20). Jeremiah too recounts the unfortunate, though just, consequences of Israel's covenant unfaithfulness against God. In terms utilizing the father–son metaphor, God says: "'I thought how I would set you among my sons, and give you a pleasant land, a heritage most beauteous of all nations. And I thought you would call me, My Father, and would not turn from following me'" (Jer 3:19, RSV).[14]

God's parental punishment of son Israel eventually culminates in exile (Jer 52). Nevertheless, even before the end of exile dawns, Jeremiah sounds prophecy of God's faithfulness and mercy engendering Israel's repentance and contrition with the effect of hope and restoration (Jer 30–32). God reaffirms sonship (and Divine Parenthood) with affectionate statements. Jeremiah 31, specifically, draws out the sonship theme and God's love.

12. *Grumbling* is a motif in the wilderness wandering narratives. See Numbers 14:2, 27, 29, 36; 16:11, 41; 17:5, 10; cf. Exodus 15:24; 16:2, 7–9, 12; 17:3.

13. The anger of the LORD is also a motif in Numbers. See Numbers 11:1, 10, 33; 12:9; 25:4; 32:10, 13–14; cf. Numbers 14:18.

14. Cf. DeRoche, "Israel's Love for God," 371.

> With weeping they shall come, and with consolations I will lead them back, I will make them walk by brooks of water, in a straight path in which they shall not stumble; for I am a father to Israel, and Ephraim is my first-born. . . . Is Ephraim my dear son? Is he my darling child? For as often as I speak against him, I do remember him still. Therefore my heart yearns for him; I will surely have mercy on him, says the LORD. (Jer 31:9, 20, RSV)

Most translations render God's emotionality in terms of how God's "heart yearns" for God's son (e.g., RSV, ESV, NIV, NASB); the idiom, though, is "internal organs murmur" (Heb. *hāmû mēʿay*), which conveys "the *thrill* of deep-felt compassion or sympathy"[15] (see also Song 5:4; Isa 16:11; cf. Isa 63:15; Jer 4:19). It is this compassion or sympathy of God which catalyzes merciful action, namely the restoration of (son) Israel after a period of chastisement in exile (cf. also Hos 11:5–6, 10–11).[16]

3.3 Israel's King as Son of God

Whereas the whole of the Israelites is personified as God's son (3.1, 3.2), one human representative is, alternatively, also metaphorically depicted as the very son of God: the king. In a covenant with David, God promises an everlasting kingly dynasty through the lineage of David. The divine appointment of a king to lead God's chosen people is expressed in terms of a father–son relationship. This generational, relational aspect is evident in the following excerpt of God's discourse.

> When your days are fulfilled and you lie down with your ancestors, I will raise up your offspring after you, who shall come forth from your body, and I will establish

15. BDB 242 (italics original). *HALOT* 1:250: "to be restless, to be turbulent" (bold original).

16. The rebellion or rebellious nature of (son) Israel is prolifically recorded elsewhere in the Bible, such as Isaiah (e.g., Isa 1:2; 30:1, 9; 48:8; 63:10; cf. Darr, *Isaiah's Vision*, 54–74); although, this passage has the most explicit references to Israel's sonship in correlation with the issue of rebellion.

> his kingdom. He shall build a house for my name, and I will establish the throne of his kingdom forever. I will be a father to him, and he shall be a son to me. When he commits iniquity, I will punish him with a rod such as mortals use, with blows inflicted by human beings. . . . Your house and your kingdom shall be made sure forever before me; your throne shall be established forever. (2 Sam 7:12–14, 16, NRSV; see also 1 Chr 17:11–14)

Furthermore, God's Messiah was eventually to materialize from the kingly Davidic lineage as the King of kings (Ps 132); additionally, the Messiah was believed to have a priestly capacity and lineage (Ps 110). The Messiah of God, accordingly, is considered the son of God (cf. Ps 89:26–27). In a preeminent messianic psalm, Psalm 2 avows: "I have set my king on Zion, my holy hill. . . . You are my son; today I have begotten you" (vv. 6, 7b, NRSV). Zion/Jerusalem is the location of the temple of YHWH God and the palace of the monarch (see further chapter 4, 4.2).

3.4 Jesus as God's Firstborn Son, True Israel, Davidic King

In the New Testament, the incarnation of Jesus reveals the very Son of God, True Israel personified, and the ultimate son of David: the King of kings, the Messiah.[17]

3.4.1 Conception and Birth of Jesus

Jesus as God's Son is first seen at conception. Luke's Gospel relays how the overshadowing of the Holy Spirit makes possible the impregnation of the virgin Mary (Luke 1:26–38). With divine seed (so to speak) and human egg, a God-human is born in Jesus of Nazareth. Such a composition is entirely anomalous and unique, and something long anticipated (cf. Gen 3:14–15). Since the fall, God's promised redeemer will cancel sin, defeat death, and reverse

17. Cf. Vellanickal, *Divine Sonship*, 9–27.

the curse's effects throughout all of creation; and this would be catalyzed by mean of a *seed*/offspring from *woman* who would crush Satan (and be crushed by Satan). This is fulfilled in Jesus' death (received strike), resurrection (strike blown), and ascension; for, truly, only a God-human could achieve such a feat.

In Matthew's Gospel, the birth of Jesus is cast in terms of the advent of the Savior (Matt 1:21). Significantly, when Herod's genocidal edict goes forth—a parallel of Pharaoh's death-edict in Exodus 1—Mary and Joseph are instructed by an angel to escape to Egypt (Matt 2:13–14). There is a parallel between Jesus entering and exiting Egypt (in Matthew) and the Israelites' eisodus and exodus from Egypt (in Exodus). Later, when God directed Joseph and family to return to the land of Israel, the author conveys the journey of the holy family thusly: "This fulfilled what the Lord had spoken through the prophet: I have called my son out of Egypt" (Matt 2:15, CEB). So,

> Matthew contrasts Jesus as the 'son' (2:15) with Hosea's 'son' (11:1). The latter who came out of Egypt was not obedient, and was judged but would be restored (11:2-11), while the former did what Israel should have done: Jesus came out of Egypt, was perfectly obedient, did not deserve judgment but suffered it anyway for guilty Israel and the world in order to restore them to God.[18]

The aspect of Jesus replaying Israel's history, as the personification of Israel, and redeeming it at every point along the way—by means of his perfect obedience to God—will be developed further (see 3.4.3).

3.4.2 Jesus as Son of God

John 3:16 famously attests that Jesus is God's one and only Son, making Jesus a firstborn as well as an only child. Indeed, in the Gospel of John a pervasive Father–Son theme features, which, in addition to revealing Jesus' relationship with God, illustrates how

18. Beale, "Hosea 11:1 in Matthew 2:15," 710.

humankind might vicariously have an analogous relationship with God in Christ.[19] In fact, the ancient, eastern ideal or goal of sonship is to become exactly like his father (cf. chapter 1, 1.5).

God's verbal (i.e., direct speech) affirmation of Jesus as God's son is disclosed at Jesus' baptism and transfiguration, as recorded in the synoptic Gospels. Upon rising from the waters of the Jordan River, "the heavens were opened to him, and he saw the Spirit of God descending like a dove and coming to rest on him; and behold, a voice from heaven said, 'This is my beloved Son, with whom I am well pleased'" (Matt 3:16b–17, ESV). Likewise, when engulfed by a heavenly cloud atop a mount, "a voice from the cloud said, 'This is my beloved Son, with whom I am well pleased; listen to him'" (Matt 17:5, ESV). In both instances, Jesus' identification as God's Son carries with it the approval and authority of God upon the life of Christ.

3.4.3 Jesus as True Israel and Obedient Son

Jesus is therefore to be understood as God's obedient son and, consequently, as true Israel.[20] This is particularly portrayed in the Gospel of Matthew, since it is Matthew who writes for a Jewish audience and who, appropriately, cites the most amount of Old Testament Scripture, in a prophecy-fulfillment manner.[21] It has already been noted that Jesus voyaging out of Egypt parallels Israel's exodus as the son of God (3.4.1),[22] yet there are several more experiences of Jesus' life that parallel Israel's history. In fact, Jesus relives and redeems Israel's history at every turn.[23]

19. Vellanickal, *Divine Sonship*, 89–225.

20. Cf. Scott, "Jesus' Vision for the Restoration of Israel," 129–43.

21. Cf. Levin, "Jesus," 415.

22. Stuart (*Exodus*, 151) notes: "God's purpose in rescuing his son [Israel from Egypt] was that his son might worship him, [and this is] a role Jesus fulfilled in his own faithful worship of the Father and a role God's people are expected to fulfill as their most basic response to his deliverance of their lives."

23. I am indebted to Scott J. Hafemann for this insight (Fall 2004 at Gordon-Conwell Theological Seminary), which is developed in this section.

When Jesus is baptized in the Jordan River (Matt 3:13–17), he is figuratively replaying the Israelites' passage through the Re(e)d Sea—passing through waters symbolizing both a renewed existence and a threshold moment marking a new era; furthermore, the Jordan is the juncture at which John the baptizer positions himself in order to hail the coming Messiah, Jesus, who enters the promised land, just as Joshua et al. entered the promised land through the parted waters of the Jordan River—in fact, Jesus and Joshua are analogous names in different languages (Gk. and Heb. respectively).[24]

When Jesus fasts for forty days and nights in the desert (Matt 4:1–11), he is figuratively and symbolically experiencing the forty years in which the Israelites wandered the wilderness (cf. 3.3.2). Moreover, Jesus redeems this segment of Israelite history by, instead of grumbling and rebelling against God and thereby sinning, not yielding to the temptations of Satan in moments of hunger and thirst to demand or accept power and kingdoms.

After reentering civilization from the desert, Jesus commences at once to preach and manifest, proclaim and demonstrate the kingdom of God through teaching, healing, restoring, and liberating (Matt 4:17, passim)—and in the establishment of a kingdom unlike earthly ones (cf. John 18:36), Jesus is upscaling Joshua's conquest and settlement of the nation of Israel in the land of Canaan; instead of militaristically battling physical enemies, Jesus spiritually advances against the kingdom of darkness by attacking and defeating Satan and its demons to effectively inaugurate the redemptive and peaceful rule of God (Matt 8:28–34; 12:22–32; cf. Col 1:13–14).

Jesus choosing twelve disciples (Matt 4:18–22) is reminiscent of God generating and establishing the twelve tribes of Israel (cf. Rev 21:9–14). Also, when Jesus ascends a mount to teach his disciples and the masses the Sermon on the Mount (Matt 5–7), Jesus is cast in the light of Moses who, likewise, ascended a mountain and brought down the law of the LORD to deliver to the people of God.

24. BDAG, 471–72.

The cited parallels are only those major analogies of Jesus as true Israel within the corpus of Matthew 1–10; yet, this is a noticeable and intentional start to the Gospel of Matthew. In the remainder of the Gospel account, Jesus is seen as the epitome of the *son of man*, an epithet especially used of Ezekiel,[25] which casts Jesus in a prophetic light.[26] In addition, the title *son of man* has messianic implications, as grounded in Daniel's prophecies (Dan 7:13; 8:17).[27] Further, as priest from a divine lineage (cf. Ps 110; Heb 5–7), Jesus fully redeems the historic life of Israel—and humanity—by dying an atoning, substitutionary death on the cross and, by Jesus' resurrection, imputes his righteousness to all who accept the Messiah's salvific redemption (cf. 2 Cor 5:21; 1 Pet 3:18).[28]

3.4.4 Jesus as King: Son of David, Son of God

Jesus is also ascribed the title *son of David* in the Gospel of Matthew (Matt 1:1, 20; 9:27; 12:23; 15:22; 20:30–31; 21:9, 15; 22:42),[29] and is ultimately understood as the King of kings, the Messiah (cf. Isa 9:6–7).[30] Not only King of the Jews (Matt 2:2; 27:11, 29, 37), Jesus is enthroned on the expiating cross,[31] ascends to the right hand of the God (Acts 1:6–11; 2:34), and enjoys perpetual coronation as king of/over all creation (Rev 4–5). Just as there are adoption overtones with God's installation of the king of Israel, so Jesus is effectively adopted by God to perform kingly/rulership (and priestly and prophetic) roles unto all humanity (see further chapter 5).

25. There are ninety-three occurrences in Ezekiel and twenty-eight occurrences in Matthew. See Kingsbury, "'Son of Man,'" 193–202.

26. Bullock, "Ezekiel," 23–31.

27. Meadowcroft, "One Like a Son of Man," 245–63.

28. Cf. Kuhn, "Son of God," 22–42.

29. In contrast, the same title in the other synoptics occurs much less frequently: Mark 10:47–48; 12:35; Luke 3:31; 18:38–39.

30. Goswell, "2 Samuel 7," 90–94; Kingsbury, "'Son of David,'" 591–602.

31. Wright, *Simply Jesus*, 173; Wright, *How God Became King*, 227.

To summarize the foregoing investigation, Israel is metaphorically personified as God's firstborn son who is called out of Egypt (or birthed by means of liberation from slavery). Personified Israel's development as an adolescent and life as an adult is generally characterized by his (via son metaphor) rebellion against God, his Divine Parent. God's son, in the Old Testament, is also indicated to be the king of Israel. Projecting into the New Testament, Jesus is the incarnate son of God; as such, Jesus redeems Israel's rebellious existence by living a perfect, righteous, and faithful life unto God. Further, as the ultimate son of man and son of David, Jesus is the promised Messiah (prophet, priest, king); as a consequence, Jesus rules sovereign, exercising perfect justice and mercy.

Israel alternatively personified as a daughter is the next facet to explore in the family of God (chapter 4). The canonical trajectory of the family of God sees its expansion as additional children are adopted by God (chapter 5); and this includes many more daughters/females as well as sons/males (chapter 6).

4

God as Parent of a Daughter

In the previous chapter, the metaphorical personification of Israel as God's son was examined. In this chapter, inversely, the metaphorical personification of Israel as God's daughter will be presented as it is advanced in the Bible. In the Old Testament, the birth and infancy of God's daughter and her prepubescent and early womanhood is developed in Ezekiel. In a multivocal manner, the prophetic metaphor portrays the Israelites also as two sisters/two daughters of God, due to the schism of the country of Israel resulting in the Northern and Southern Kingdoms. In both the Old and New Testaments, the capital city of Jerusalem, or Zion, is personified as God's daughter as well. Furthermore, in the New Testament Jesus makes a curious and endearing reference to a woman as (his?) daughter, which will be analyzed; this exchange also develops the theme of the people of God as daughter, within the larger familial biblical theology. Therefore, while the (Hebrew) Bible has devoted material on natural daughters (young and old), both in its narrative and legislative portions,[1] the present scope is limited to the biblical portrayal of the metaphoric daughter(s) of God.

1. See, e.g., Russaw, *Daughters in the Hebrew Bible*; Stiebert, *Fathers and Daughters in the Bible*; Pressler, *Women Found in the Deuteronomic Family Laws.*

To register a disclaimer, it may ostensibly seem that Israel's portrayal as a daughter is more demeaning and derogatory than Israel's metaphoric depiction as a son in the Bible; such an evaluation gives rise to disparagingly sexist conclusions to (postmodern) readers. It should be noted, however, that there are both good and bad aspects attributed to both gendered metaphors, so any and all righteousness before God has to do with covenant faithfulness (obedience) and any and all wickedness before God relates to covenant unfaithfulness (disobedience). Consequently, equity among the sexes, i.e., son Israel and daughter Israel, is tenable; this will be substantiated.

4.1 God's Daughter(s)

4.1.1 Infant and Adolescent Daughter

Ezekiel 16 is the biblical text which develops the concept of Israel as God's daughter in the greatest detail, particularly in the stages of her infancy and adolescence. Midway through Ezekiel 16 the metaphor evolves, changing from Israel as God's daughter to Israel as God's (unfaithful) wife. While it is startling to imagine marrying one's daughter, it is important that keep in mind that familial metaphors are utilized by the prophet in order to underscore the egregious sin of Israel and the tragic erosion of intimate relationship between God and God's people.

Ezekiel 16, by way of warning, might probably be the most disturbing chapter in the Bible; consequently, it has been the object of disdain and outrage of many feminist scholars.[2] Certainly while the disturbing portions cannot be overlooked or glossed, the graphic images of sexual violence, prostitution, and adultery is confined to Ezekiel 16:15–58, which exploits an alternate

2. E.g., Day, "Rhetoric and Domestic Violence," 205–30; Day, "Bitch Had It Coming to Her," 231–54; Shields, "Multiple Exposures," 5–18; Claassens, "Transforming God-Language," 1–11; Bibb, "There's No Sex in Your Violence," 337–45. Cf. Koller, "Pornography or Theology?" 402–21; Haag et al., "Ezekiel 16," 198–210. Contra, e.g., Zoutewdaw, "Grotesque Attack," 63–84.

metaphor (wife Israel) than that of the present scope. In contrast, the metaphor of Israel as God's daughter, in Ezekiel 16:1–14, reveals God's deep compassion, love, and care.

Rather than Israel being birthed by God (Deut 32:18; Isa 46:3–4), God, in Ezekiel 16, finds, takes-in, and rears daughter Israel (cf. Deut 32:9–18; Exod 4:22). God's procurement of a newborn daughter is allegorized as follows.

> Thus says the Lord GOD to Jerusalem: Your origin and your birth were in the land of the Canaanites; your father was an Amorite, and your mother a Hittite. As for your birth, on the day you were born your navel cord was not cut, nor were you washed with water to cleanse you, nor rubbed with salt, nor wrapped in cloths. No eye pitied you, to do any of these things for you out of compassion for you; but you were thrown out in the open field, for you were abhorred on the day you were born. I passed by you, and saw you flailing about in your blood. As you lay in your blood, I said to you, "Live!" . . . You grew up . . . yet you were naked and bare. I passed by you again and looked on you . . . I spread the edge of my cloak over you, and covered your nakedness . . . and you became mine. (Ezek 16:1–8, NRSV)

As an exposed and abandoned foundling, newborn Israel is perhaps hours old and hours away from death; whether by threat of natural elements, lack of nourishment, or becoming food for wild animals, infant Israel is extremely vulnerable (in the world of the narrative).[3] She is neglected and rejected (v. 5); she is still connected to her umbilical cord (and placenta?), besmeared in birth blood and besmirched in vernix caseosa (vv. 4a, 6a). Then, God, having discovered her, has compassion on this female newborn and rescues her (v. 5a)[4] and infuses her with life (v. 6b).

3. See further, Koskenniemi, *Exposure of Infants.*

4. This is not the typical term for "compassion" (*rḥm*) that we saw in chapter 3. Instead, Heb. *ḥemĕlâ* describes divine intervention unto salvation, a lifesaving mercy (see also Gen 19:16; Isa 63:9); this adverb comes from the verb *ḥml*, "to spare" (e.g., Exod 2:6). BDB 328; *HALOT* 1:328.

The spreading of God's cloak edge (Heb. *kānāp*) over the female infant is a gesture of protection, shielding her from the elements and providing relief. Theriomorphically, a similar attribute and action is ascribed to God in the form of God's wings (Heb. *kānāp*) providing refuge for the God-fearer. For example, Boaz says to Ruth, "'May the LORD reward you for your deeds, and may you have a full reward from the LORD, the God of Israel, under whose wings [*kānāp*] you have come for refuge!'" (Ruth 2:12, NRSV). Similarly, the psalmist attests: "How precious is your steadfast love, O God! All people may take refuge in the shadow of your wings [*kānāp*]" (Ps 36:7, NRSV). Thus, God protects whilst providing.

Continuing the metaphor, the prophet, from the perspective of God, elaborates the care and provision given as daughter Israel grows into adolescence and (pubescent) young adulthood.

> Then I bathed you with water and washed off the blood from you, and anointed you with oil. I clothed you with embroidered cloth and with sandals of fine leather; I bound you in fine linen and covered you with rich fabric. I adorned you with ornaments: I put bracelets on your arms, a chain on your neck, a ring on your nose, earrings in your ears, and a beautiful crown upon your head. You were adorned with gold and silver, while your clothing was of fine linen, rich fabric, and embroidered cloth. You had choice flour and honey and oil for food. You grew exceedingly beautiful, fit to be a queen. Your fame spread among the nations on account of your beauty, for it was perfect because of my splendor that I had bestowed on you, says the Lord GOD. (Ezek 16:9–14, NRSV)

As a parent, God lavishes attention and gifts upon daughter Israel; fine clothing, plenteous jewelry, gourmet foods, and privilege and status before neighboring peoples are all the niceties God bestowed upon Israel. These gifts are, unfortunately, later squandered by daughter Israel, and her person is denigrated in the most scandalous of ways—namely, sex and violence (see Ezek 16:15–58). Amy Kalmanofsky rightly states that "the prophets' rhetoric of horror [is] designed to terrify their audience into reform."[5] To this end, the balance of Ezekiel 16 signals the Israelites' covenantal unfaithfulness through the metaphor of prostitution, etc.; nonetheless, the biblical chapter closes with a testament of the faithfulness of God and the hope of redemption for Israel (Ezek 16:59–63).

4.1.2 God's Adult Daughters

Whereas Ezekiel 16:1–14 metaphorically depicts Israel as a daughter of God and Ezekiel 16:15–58 metaphorically depicts Israel as God's wife, Ezekiel 23 portrays something similar. The allegory of Ezekiel 23 renders God as having two sister wives, and these sisters are naturally also daughters. Though the metaphor shifts quite significantly from Ezekiel 16 to Ezekiel 23, the remaining similarities between the two allegories, nonetheless, loosely connotes God having two daughters, sisters as they are.[6]

The overture to the parable of Ezekiel 23 reads:

> The word of the LORD came to me: Mortal, there were two women, the daughters of one mother; they played the whore in Egypt; they played the whore in their youth; their breasts were caressed there, and their virgin bosoms were fondled. Oholah was the name of the elder and Oholibah the name of her sister. They became mine, and they bore sons and daughters. As for their names, Oholah is Samaria, and Oholibah is Jerusalem. (Ezek 23:1–4, NRSV)

In addition to the internal interpretive keys within the text, a few other elements need to be decoded. First, the same mother of the daughters refers to the common origins of the sisters in Egypt and/or their shared existence as a former united monarchy (1050–930 BCE).[7] Second, upon the schism of the nation (930

5. Kalmanofsky, "Dangerous Sisters," 300.

6. For various overlapping familial imagery lending to alternative perspectives, see Jacobs, "Ezekiel 16," 201–2; cf. Stiebert, *Fathers and Daughters*, 199–201.

7. In both Ezekiel 16 and 23 Israel's (figuratively) biological parents are

BCE), Israel divides into two kingdoms: the northern kingdom of Samaria/Israel (930–722 BCE) and the southern kingdom of Judah (930–586 BCE), or Oholah and Oholibah respectively.[8] Third, just as Ezekiel casts the two kingdoms as two females/daughters (Ezek 23; cf. 16:45–58), so similarly Jeremiah renders the Northern and Southern Kingdoms as two males/sons (Jer 31:9); indeed, the association of nations as progeny of their divine patron is a commonplace feature in antiquity.[9]

As with Ezekiel 16, the remainder of Ezekiel 23 graphically and thoroughly delineates the consistency and vile nature of the sisters' sexual depravity. Sexual adultery is a metaphor for covenant unfaithfulness, i.e., disobedience to the law of the LORD. Thus, Ezekiel 23 theologically commentates on the exile, how it came about and the meaning thereof.

4.1.3 God's Punishment of Daughter (and Son) Israel

All the atrocities outlined in Ezekiel 16 and 23 of God's daughter(s) refer to Israel's covenantal unfaithfulness, and the punishments (curses) of such transgressions were stipulated by God in Deuteronomy 28. Covenantal unfaithfulness is alternately expressed in the metaphors of son Israel and daughter Israel: (metaphorically personified) son Israel is recalcitrantly rebellious (see chapter 3) and (metaphorically personified) daughter Israel is brazenly licentious (chapter 4). According to the law of the LORD, the penalty for both the (natural) rebellious son (Deut 21:18–21) and the

either cryptically referenced (Ezek 16:3, 45) or alluded to (Ezek 23:2–3a; cf. Exod 4:22–23a); and this intimates God's custody of Israel is one of an adoptive parent (see chapter 5).

8. "Oholah has usually been interpreted as 'her tent' (= sanctuary, as in Ps 15:1; 61:5) . . . in contrast with Oholibah, taken to mean 'my tent [is] in her' . . . These putatively symbolic names are supposed to refer respectively to the illegitimate, unauthorized sanctuaries of the northern, Samarian kingdom (I Kings 12:28ff.; 'the calf of Samaria,' Hos 8:6) and to the authorized Jerusalem Temple" (Greenberg, *Ezekiel 21–37*, 474).

9. Maier, *Daughter Zion, Mother Zion*, 61–74. Cf. also Dearman, "Daughter Zion and Her Place in God's Household," 144–59.

(natural) promiscuous daughter (Deut 22:13–30) is death. Therefore, whether metaphorically personified as a son or daughter of God with each corresponding depravity, the nation of Israel was confronted with its own figurative death, in the form of exile, due to covenantal disobedience (Lev 26:33–44; Deut 28:36–41, 63–68).

4.2 Daughter Zion/Jerusalem

"In biblical texts about Jerusalem," Christl Maier explains, "the literary device of personification attaches a female body to the place, a body that is a spatial concept and at the same time a personal category defining the relationship of the place to the people living in it."[10] Consequently, Jerusalem, referred to not only as a female but as a daughter, extends the metaphor of God's daughter in the Bible. Daughter Zion (Jerusalem) is a pseudonym utilized in both the Old and New Testaments.

4.2.1 Old Testament

Zion, an ancient term that refers to (parts of) Jerusalem (2 Sam 5:6–8), indicates the country's capital city and the location of the temple.[11] Common among the biblical occurrences of *Zion* is its appositional relationship with *daughter*, yielding the personification of (God's) Daughter Zion.[12] Christl Maier elucidates,

> A city provides the main sources of life such as food, shelter, and a home to the people, just as a mother for her children. . . . Therefore, in religious discourse the daughter metaphor provides a means to talk about the relationship between the population of the city and its patron deity. . . . Thus, Daughter Zion conflates the city space and its population into a personified woman who

10. Maier, *Daughter Zion, Mother Zion*, 28.

11. Mare, "Zion," 6:1096–97.

12. See Follis, "Zion, Daughter of," 6:1103; Conway, "Daughter Zion," 101–26.

> is loved and protected by YHWH like a daughter by a father.[13]

Furthermore, *daughter of Zion* is most prolifically attested in poetic and prophetic biblical material generated in the exilic to postexilic eras. This literary phenomenon indicates grief at the destruction of Jerusalem; and, perhaps it suggests as well a nostalgic appreciation for God's special relationship with Judahites (Israelites), as represented by the capital city which housed the temple (cf. 2 Sam 7). Johanna Stiebert summarizes the use and function of *Daughter Zion* in Lamentations—the highest concentration of the alias in any biblical book—stating:

> In the feminized Jerusalem-daughter-of-God passages of Lamentations the prevailing mood is one of sadness for the glory of Jerusalem that is now replaced by devastating destruction and profound suffering. There *is* mention of Jerusalem's sin (1:8) and her uncleanness (a metaphor for transgression?) clinging to her skirts (1:8–9), even of her accountability and submission to punishment (1:18, 20, 22), but the references to sin are trumped by the considerably more prevalent and considerably more vivid and dramatic images of suffering.[14]

At the end of the seventy-year exile (Jer 25:11-13; Dan 9:2 [586–515 BCE]), the Judeans were liberated at the hand of King Cyrus of the Persian Empire, who toppled the Babylonian Empire (Ezra 1:1–4; 2 Chr 36:22–23). In the exilic and post-exilic eras, God relentlessly pursues God's daughter; moreover, God forgives and atones for Daughter Zion's past transgressions so thoroughly that virginity, i.e., innocence or righteousness, is again ascribed to Israel.[15] Jeremiah's prophetic statements are representative of this.

13. Maier, *Daughter Zion, Mother Zion*, 73, 74.

14. Stiebert, *Fathers and Daughters*, 190 (emphasis original). Stiebert (*Fathers and Daughters*, 192) further advances: "The metaphor is effective because the daughter is vulnerable, because her punishment is disproportionate, and because she is entitled to protection from her father [i.e., YHWH]—that is what best explains and legitimizes the choice of the daughter-metaphor."

15. Within the specific context of exile, God is said to be punishing the sins

> Again, I will build you up, and you will be rebuilt, virgin Israel. Again, you will play your tambourines and dance with joy. . . . Return, virgin Israel; return to these towns of yours. How long will you hem and haw, my rebellious daughter? The LORD has created something new on earth: Virgin Israel will once again embrace her God! (Jer 31:4, 21b–22, CEB; cf. Zeph 3:14–15)[16]

A new start for the remnant in Jerusalem, and the surrounding area, is the focus of post-exilic writings (Haggai, Zechariah, Malachi, Ezra–Nehemiah, and 1–2 Chronicles), and this new era is marked by a new temple on Mount Zion—it is the second temple period (516 BCE—70 CE). In this setting, another Daughter Zion prophecy is anticipated, one which also realizes an approaching kingly figure. The prophet Zechariah foresees the following: "Rejoice greatly, Daughter Zion. Sing aloud, Daughter Jerusalem. Look, your king will come to you. He is righteous and victorious. He is humble and riding . . . on a colt, the offspring of a donkey" (Zech 9:9, CEB).

4.2.2 New Testament

In his so-called triumphal entry, Jesus ascends Mount Zion to approach the (second) temple in Jerusalem for the commencement of the Festival of Passover. Jesus makes his transit upon a donkey's colt, to—as the Gospel writers advance—fulfill what is prophesied in Zechariah 9:9.

---

of the covenant people twice over (Isa 40:2) and, alternately, seven times over (Lev 26:18, 21, 24, 28). For her discussion of virginity in Levantine and biblical literature, see Russaw, *Daughters*, 5–13.

16. In the previous chapter, Jeremiah 31:(9) 20 was cited to illustrate the (divine) parent-son metaphor; and, here, in the verses immediately following, Jeremiah 31:21–22, the (divine) parent-daughter metaphor is utilized. Such is the interchangeable, multivalent, and poetic use of scriptural language (cf. Stiebert, *Fathers and Daughters*, 189; Maier, *Daughter Zion, Mother Zion*, 73). See also Stiebert, *Fathers and Daughters*, 201–4.

- "Tell the daughter of Zion, Look, your king is coming to you, humble, and mounted on a donkey, and on a colt, the foal of a donkey" (Matt 21:5, NRSV).
- "Do not be afraid, daughter of Zion. Look, your king is coming, sitting on a donkey's colt!" (John 12:15, NRSV).

Thus, Matthew and John cite Zechariah and draw from the Old Testament tradition of personified Israel—or symbolized Zion—as God's daughter. While Luke does not quote Zechariah 9:9 in his Gospel account, the third evangelist does allude to Daughter Zion. Carrying his cross on the way to Golgotha, Jesus addressed the "women who were beating their breasts and wailing for him" and said, "'Daughters of Jerusalem, do not weep for me, but weep for yourselves and for your children'" (Luke 23:27b, 28b, NRSV).[17] That this reference emanates from Jesus is poignant for it evokes a parent–daughter relationship (see 4.3).

The kingly figure in Zechariah 9:9 purports a messianic role in its New Testament appropriation (cf. Pss 2, 110). Furthermore, Zion traditions of kingship and enthronement are resonant in the passion narrative(s), for Jesus, as the son of David and the son of God, is enthroned (as it were) upon the cross on Mount Zion.[18] This is typologically suggestive of God coming again—this time in the incarnate Christ—to rescue God's daughter.

4.3 Jesus'/God's "Daughter"?

Aside from its sparse and elusive references to the Zion tradition (see previous section), the metaphor of God's daughter is rather absent in the New Testament. Only a couple extrapolations of the metaphorical motif can be made; and, corroborating the Old Testament (via canonical criticism), these extrapolations both find their crux in Ezekiel 16 (see 4.1). First, whereas Ezekiel 16 sees a foundling become God's daughter and then bride (in the complex, evolving metaphor), the New Testament likewise describes

17. See Soards, "Jesus' Speech to the 'Daughters of Jerusalem,'" 241–44.

18. Levenson, "Zion Traditions," 6:1098–102.

the new covenant people of God as God's children (daughters and sons) and as God's bride, the bride of Christ (see Eph 5:29–32; Rev 19:1–8; 21:1–10; 22:17). Second, the stage of Ezekiel 16 which depicts Israel singularly as God's daughter finds some syntactical parallels with a healing account in the synoptic Gospels.

As Jesus is *en route* to heal the twelve-year-old daughter of Jairus, a woman suffering from hemorrhaging for twelve years is healed by reaching out and touching Jesus' garment. When he thence speaks with her, Jesus addresses the woman—in an unparalleled manner—as (his) daughter (Matt 9:22; Mark 5:34; Luke 8:48; cf. Luke 13:16; 23:28); this is especially provocative since she may be older than Jesus is.[19] Jesus' interaction with this woman, moreover, can be seen (canonically) as a redemption of the foundling daughter in Ezekiel 16, as the following graph parallels.

Ezekiel 16 allegory	**Jesus heals a woman**
I passed by you, and saw you flailing about in your [birth] <u>blood</u>. As you lay in your <u>blood</u> . . . (Ezek 16:6, NRSV)	A woman was there who had been subject to <u>bleeding</u> for twelve years, but no one could heal her. (Luke 8:43, NRSV)
I spread <u>the edge of my cloak</u> over you. (Ezek 16:8a, NRSV)	She came up behind him and touched <u>the edge of his cloak</u>, and immediately her bleeding stopped. (Luke 8:44, NRSV)
. . . I said to you, 'Live!' (Ezek 16:6b); . . . and you became mine. (Ezek 16:8b, NRSV)	Then he said to her, "Daughter, your faith has healed you. Go in peace." (Luke 8:48, NRSV)

In each biblical text there is: (1) a vulnerable female having an issue with/of blood, (2) the edge of God's figurative cloak or Jesus' actual cloak providing both/either protection and/or restoration, and (3) God/Jesus bidding the female—as (his) daughter—to live, to enjoy an extension and fullness of life.[20] The figurative rescue in

19. So, e.g., Bock, *Luke*, 1:798. See further Soskice, *Kindness of God*, 92–97.

20. "God in Christ says to his children, 'Live!' And because he's the God who refuses to let even our rankest sin derail his determined plan to save us, we can know that we *will* live with this God forever" (Hoezee, "Live!," 91; emphasis original).

Ezekiel 16 and the literal healing in Luke 8 bi-optically portrays the multidimensionality of God's salvation: it is both physical and spiritual, corporeal and incorporeal, earthly and ethereal.[21]

To review, God as the parent of a daughter has been developed. God's actions exerted toward God's daughter include rescuing her by means of protection and providing refuge; also, daughter Israel is graciously and lavishly provided for in terms of affluence and honor (Ezek 16:1–14). Upon her adulthood, daughter Israel becomes degenerate in covenantal disobedience (Ezek 16 and 23); nevertheless, her Divine Parent relentless pursues wayward Israel unto restoration. Daughter Zion, a poetic and symbolic variation of Israel personified metaphorically as God's daughter, pays for her sins through suffering exile (Lamentations) and is thereby acquitted by God; as a result, God declares Israel innocent (*virgin Israel*) and deems her righteous (Jer 31). Daughter Zion eventually meets her king in Jesus of Nazareth (Zech 9:9; cited in Matt 21:5; John 12:15). Jesus, moreover, occasionally speaks of Israelite women as (his) daughter; specifically, a woman receives healing from Jesus via touching (in faith) his cloak (Luke 8), a narrative reminiscent of the Ezekiel 16 allegory.

The Divine Parent enfolds many more children into the family of God; this is done by means of divine adoption in Christ Jesus (chapter 5). Life within the family of God is fleshed out, thence (chapter 6).

21. There are many beautiful variegated ways in which females are validated and honored by Jesus in the Gospels and how the equity of females is contended for by the early church as represented in the rest of the New Testament. However, the present scope—namely, the metaphor of God's daughter—restricts elaboration upon these important matters.

5

God as Adopter of Children

IN THE PREVIOUS TWO chapters, it was examined how God is portrayed—especially in the Old Testament—as a parent of an only son, on the one hand (chapter 3), and a daughter, on the other (chapter 4). Despite the metaphors being straightforward, however, even these instances both invoke the concept of adoption. In the case of son Israel, he is already living in slavery; then God *called* his son Israel out of Egypt (Exod 4:22; Hos 11:1). For a *paterfamilias* to pronounce someone as one's child and to rear that child as one's own is typical of adoption rites and practices.[1] In the case of daughter Israel, similarly, she is exposed and abandoned for dead by her parents (Ezek 16:3–5), yet God elects to rescue her, bids her to live, and says that she will be God's (Ezek 16:6–8). This too is reminiscent of adoption practice, for the one who saves an abandoned child from death and raises that child *ipso facto* becomes the adoptive parent.[2] Nevertheless, the Old Testament lacks legislation expressly mandating or explicating the institution of adoption; rather, what is present as a loose equivalent is levirate marriage and kinsmen redemption.[3] Instead, the notion of biblical adoption comes into focus in the New Testament.

1. Cf. Melnyk, "When Israel Was a Child," 249–58.

2. Cf. Malul, "Adoption of Foundlings in the Bible," 97–126.

3. See Lyall, "Roman Law," 79–95; Longenecker, "Metaphor of Adoption," 72.

Initially in this chapter, a survey is presented of God's propensity, in the Old Testament, to effectively adopt (i.e., protect and provide for) orphans. Tracing the adoption theme into the New Testament, there is allusion that Jesus himself is adopted by God. Ultimately, though, the Triune God's redemptive work and activity in the salvation of humanity is portrayed metaphorically as an adoption process and its pursuant familial relationship: God Almighty orchestrates the adoption plan, Jesus Christ pays the adoption price with his life, and the Holy Spirit's indwelling presence in adopted children of God is the deposit ensuring the adoption. Subsequently, there are a variety of benefits enjoyed by adopted children of God, as legitimate heirs, which are examined; by juxtaposing the Old and New Testaments, the scale and scope of what the Triune God grants new covenant adoptees in terms of inheritance is staggering and spectacular. Finally, the simple truth and beautiful reality of people saved by grace through faith in Christ being children of God is presented.

5.1 God's Immense Compassion for Orphans (and Widows and Immigrant)

There are not many instances of natural adoption in the Old Testament; these individuals include Eliezer (Gen 15:2–4), Ephraim and Manasseh (Gen 48:5), Moses (Exod 2:10), and Esther (Esth 2:7, 15).[4] Nevertheless, in a spiritual and theological sense God figuratively and effectively adopts individuals for authoritative roles; for example, David is effectively adopted as king (2 Sam 7:14; 1 Chr 17:13) and the nation of Israel is adopted as God's agent in the world (Jer 3:19; 31:9; cf. Deut 7:6–7; 14:1–2).[5]

Furthermore, it is revealing that God has an immense compassion for orphans; and God protects and provides, directly

4. Bartlett, "Adoption in the Bible," 381–84; Rossell, "New Testament Adoption," 233–34. Cf. Levin ("Jesus," 423) who also adds Naomi's adoption of Ruth's child, Obed (and an apocryphal example in Tobit).

5. Melnyk, "When Israel Was a Child," 248–51; Scott, *Adoption*, 100–117; Bartlett, "Adoption in the Bible," 376–81; Burke, *Adopted*, 47–86.

and indirectly (i.e., through humans and creation), for these persons—which is the responsibility of an adoptive parent. In fact, a prominent motif in the legislation of the Sinaitic Covenant is the provision and protection for society's most vulnerable peoples—namely, widows, orphans, and immigrants (Exod 22:21–22; Deut 10:18; 14:29; 16:11, 14; 24:17, 19–21; 26:12–13; 27:19).[6] Below are just a few scriptural examples of dozens which underscore God's immense compassion for orphans (as part of the aforementioned triadic grouping).

- "Leave me your orphans, and I'll look after them" (Jer 49:11a, CEB);
- "Father of orphans . . . is God in his holy habitation" (Ps 68:5, CEB);
- "You [God] are the orphan's helper" (Ps 10:14b, CEB);
- "In you [God] the orphan finds compassion" (Hos 14:3b, CEB).

Whether in the mouth of God or ascribed of God by the psalmist or prophet, God is the defender of the defenseless, the parent-like figure to orphans.

Turning to the New Testament, both the figurative and metaphorical expressions of the adoption theme are present and further developed.

5.2 Jesus and Adoption: The Gospels

5.2.1 Jesus of Nazareth adopted by God Almighty

In one sense Joseph is Jesus' adoptive father,[7] since he was not involved in the child's conception; Joseph takes impregnated Mary to be his wife and supports both her and the baby (cf. chapter 3).

6. Brueggemann, "Vulnerable Children," 411–12; Sneed, "Alien, Orphan, and Widow," 498–507.

7. Globe, "Matthew 1 and Luke 2," 62; Bartlett, "Adoption in the Bible," 386–87.

Alternatively, in another sense, God may be portrayed as adopting Jesus (back) upon his baptism.[8] This tension and interplay, presented in the synoptic Gospels, is fascinating, and it is advantageous in understanding divine adoption.[9]

At Jesus' baptism, the heavens tear open, the Holy Spirit descends as a dove and rests upon Jesus, and the voice of God Almighty declares, "'You are my Son, the Beloved; with you I am well pleased' (Mark 1:11, NRSV; Matt 3:17; Luke 3:22; cf. Mark 9:7; Matt 17:5; Luke 9:35). Scholars note how this utterance mimics adoption formula (cf. Ps 2:7);[10] if so, what this biblical vignette conveys is Jesus' divine adoption. This means that Jesus, at this point in his life, transitions away from the obligations of leading his biological family and is transferred to God's family, to be the leader of it. The contrast between the two families surfaces throughout the Jesus' life.

Once when Jesus was teaching in a packed-out house, a message was relayed to him that his mother and brothers and sisters were outside wanting to talk with him (Matt 12:46–50; Mark 3:31–35; Luke 8:19–21). This brief and remote exchange seems to insinuate that Jesus was being beckoned to lead his biological family, for there is an allusion in the close context of the narrative that Joseph is deceased (Matt 13:55–56).[11] If so, Jesus as the eldest (half) brother, who was undoubtably apprenticed by Joseph as a carpenter, was to lead the family and the family trade in Joseph's absence. Jesus takes this opportunity to respond not to his biological family but to his redefined, spiritual family.

> [Jesus] replied, "Who are my mother and my brothers?" And looking at those who sat around him, he said, ". . .

8. Bartlett, "Adoption in the Bible," 385–86.

9. Levin ("Jesus," 432) states that in Matthew and Luke "there is the idea . . . that Jesus retained the lineage of both his 'fathers': he remained 'Son of God', while also claiming the status of his 'adopted' Davidic heritage." Cf. also Peppard, "Adopted and Begotten," 93–94.

10. Bartlett, "Adoption in the Bible," 385–88; Cf. Scott, *Adoption*, 100–17; Melnyk, "When Israel Was a Child," 250. See further Burke, *Adopted*, 102–07.

11. Cf. van Aarde, "The Carpenter's Son (Mt 13:55)," 186–88.

> Whoever does the will of God is my brother and sister and mother." (Mark 3:33–35, NRSV; cf. Luke 11:27–28)

In an analogous passage, Jesus instructed "call no one your father on earth, for you have one Father—the one in heaven" (Matt 23:9, NRSV). Taken together, God's family comprises of a Divine Parent and all other familial members are children, those who do (i.e., perform, enact, materialize) God's will (cf. Matt 6:9b–10).[12]

Surely not all of this was realized at the time Jesus' biological family came to him, though. The ostensible act of snubbing family is a great affront in Eastern cultures, and to redefine the family unit is scandalous. Nevertheless, Jesus is leading—as the true elder brother (cf. Rom 8:29; Heb 2:11–12, 17)—a family of divine origin, because he has been adopted by YHWH God at his baptism.[13] Moreover, since every family had a trade, the trade of family of God is discipleship, making disciples of Christ (Matt 28:19–20), or, metaphorically speaking, God's family trade is adoption, lovingly bringing orphaned and/or estranged sons and daughters (back) into the family of God (see 5.3).

5.2.2 Jesus as Adoption Agent of God Almighty

Whereas the synoptic Gospels record Jesus effectively becoming adopted by God and thence leading the family of God, the Gospel of John presents an alternative perspective on and a more explicit reference to adoption. At the top of his Farewell Discourse (John 14–17), Jesus, when announcing his departure, consoles his disciples by ensuring them that they will not be orphaned. "'I won't leave you as orphans. I will come to you'" (John 14:18, CEB). What does this mean, and how will Jesus adopt?

Jesus explains, "'My Father's house has room to spare. If that weren't the case, would I have told you that I'm going to prepare a place for you? When I go to prepare a place for you, I will return

12. Cf. Gundry, "Children in the Gospel of Mark," 168.

13. Cogently, the sign of being part of the family of God is also the believer's baptism—like Jesus.

and take you to be with me so that where I am you will be too'" (John 14:2–3, CEB). The Gk. term for God's house, or household, is *oikia/oikos*,[14] and the many dwelling places (Gk. *monē*) has typically been understood as rooms or suites within the household structure. Clarification of these two terms will enhancement understanding of the household-adoption illustration in John 14.

The word "dwellings" (Gk. *menō/monē*) in John 14–15 conveys a relational reality more than it does, say, heavenly mansions (as per the Tyndale and KJV translations).[15] This same lexeme is used frequently in its close literary context.

- Father *dwells* in Jesus (14:10)
- Holy Spirit *dwells* with believers (14:17)
- Father and Son make *dwelling* with the believer (14:23)
- Jesus *dwells* within believers (14:25)
- Believers and Jesus *dwell* within one another (15:4–7)
- Believers *dwell* in Jesus and his word (15:9–10)

"Could it be clearer from context that the first thing we are to think of when reading, 'In my Father's house are many μοναὶ [*monai*],' is not mansions in the sky, but spiritual positions in Christ . . . ?"[16] After begging the rhetorical question upon the scriptural witness, Robert Gundry then deduced, "[t]he father's house is no longer heaven, but God's household or family" on earth presently![17] This does not diminish the meaning of the promise, however; instead, it bolsters Jesus' assurance.[18] For, the Christian's hope is not something unseen and far away, but, rather, God drawing close and materializing God's presence in the unity of believers (John 17:23). Therefore, instead of an orphanage or a home in a distant

14. *Ikea* is a term that comes from *oikia/oikos*—it is natural that Ikea is a store which sells all imaginable items for the home.

15. See BDAG, 658.

16. Gundry, "*Monai*," 70.

17. Gundry, "*Monai*," 70.

18. See Wright, *Surprised By Hope*.

and delayed place, God's presence by the Holy Spirit resides within adopted children (e.g., Rom 8:9–11; 1 Cor 3:16; 6:19; cf. 2 Cor 12:9; Eph 3:17).[19]

Turning attention to the other key term in John 14:2–3, *oikos*, the backdrop of ancient Mediterranean household structures—both familial and architectural—is essential to properly interpreting Jesus' teaching.[20]

> Throughout the Mediterranean world there existed several housing types, which promoted this type of communal living. Ancient society . . . had multiply generations living in one household. In addition to the social makeup of the houses involving multigenerations [of family members], slaves, free workers, and clients likewise lived under the same roof.[21]

In the household codes of the New Testament (Eph 5:21–6:9; Col 3:18–25), the husband-wife, parents-children, and masters-slaves binaries are all addressed together precisely because they all lived under the same roof (*oikos*).[22] Thus, the average household (*oikos*) was about twelve to fifteen persons who occupied various rooms (*monai*).[23]

The apostle Paul, in texts like Ephesians 5:21–6:9 and Colossians 3:18–25, instructs the christological reshaping of relationships within the household unit as befitting the family of God.[24] For the first three centuries of its existence, the church met in

19. Howard-Brook, *Becoming Children of God*, 313–15.

20. BDAG, 698–99. Coloe ("Temple Imagery in John," 375) explains, "the phrase 'in my Father's house' should be interpreted in the light of its earlier usage where 'my Father's house' referred to the Jerusalem temple (2:16). Jesus' use of the phrase 'my Father's house' to refer to a building is quite strange. In the Hebrew Scriptures, 'my father's house' always means the group of people who make up the household, such as the family and servants, or even the future descendants."

21. Ermatinger, *World of Ancient Rome*, 1:418; cf. Dever, *Lives of Ordinary People in Ancient Israel*, 186–88.

22. Cf. Ferguson, *Backgrounds*, 71.

23. Cf. Das, "1 Corinthians 11:17–34 Revisited," 193.

24. See e.g., Dudrey, "Submit Yourselves to One Another," 27–44.

homes (house churches); thus, it was the household unit (*oikos*) that was foundational to the establishment and growth of the early church.[25] This is attested in Acts and is further borne out until the time of Emperor Constantine, predominantly.[26]

Jesus, even prior to his adoption reference in John 14, alluded to a new household of God where peripheral persons are brought close into the family proper. Jesus had proclaimed: "'The slave does not have a permanent place in the household [*oikia*]; the son has a place there forever. So if the Son makes you free, you will be free indeed'" (John 8:35–36, NRSV). While drawing on the (literal) household institution, Jesus' meaning is (metaphorically) spiritual: all are servants to sin until the Son of God liberates people and enfold them into the divine family. It is for this reason that the author of Hebrews similarly claims, "Christ . . . was faithful over God's house [*oikos*] as a son, and we are his house [*oikos*] if we hold firm the confidence and the pride that belong to hope" (Heb 3:6, NRSV; cf. Eph 2:19, 22).

So, when Jesus tells his disciples, "'I won't leave you as orphans. I will come to you'" (John 14:18, CEB), how does Jesus achieve this adoption, since adopting orphans is the role of a parent?[27] It has been proffered (see 5.2.1) that Jesus himself is adopted as the Son of God and consequently serves as the elder brother of the family of God.[28] Yet sonship and brotherhood focus primarily on the human aspect of Jesus' personage; as the Messiah of God, Jesus—as the face of the Father (John 14:8–9; 2 Cor 4:6)—also operates as the head of the household of God (cf. Col 1:18a). Jesus' role and function as divine adopter is developed in the Epistles.[29]

25. See White, "Paul and *Pater Familias*," 457–87; Banks, *Paul's Idea of Community*.

26. See e.g., Shelley, *Church History*, 45–119.

27. Jesus is ostensibly using adoption formulae in the act giving John and Mary to one another as son and mother (see Lyall, "Roman Law," 463).

28. So Heim, *Adoption*, 249.

29. Peppard ("Adopted and Begotten," 92–110) observes that whereas in the Gospel of John Jesus is adopted and Christians are begotten, it is the opposite in the Pauline epistles; in those letters, Jesus is begotten of God and Christians are adopted.

5.3 The Triune God is in the Adoption Business: The Epistles

There are five references to adoption in the (Pauline) epistles (Rom 8:15, 23; 9:4; Gal 4:5; Eph 1:5).[30] What is striking about the utilization of this term in the New Testament is how each member of the Godhead is actively involved in the process of adoption, each playing their own crucial part in it. The ensuing investigation will appraise each occurrence of "adoption" (Gk. *huiothesia*) in the New Testament and thereby view the respective roles of the Triune God in the saving, adoption event.[31]

5.3.1 God Almighty

God Almighty initiates and orchestrates events to result in the adoption of sons and daughters for God. The opening of Ephesians eloquently proclaims: "God destined us to be his adopted children through Jesus Christ because of his love. This was according to his goodwill and plan" (Eph 1:5, CEB). The impetus for God's adoption act is love (cf. also John 3:16)! Similarly stated in another epistle, Paul asserts, "when the fulfillment of the time came, God sent his Son, born through a woman, and born under the Law. This was so he could redeem those under the Law so that we could be adopted" (Gal 4:4–5, CEB). God catalyzing redemption, or adoption, seamlessly segues into the person and work of Jesus, the Messiah; for, "[t]he purpose of God's sending Jesus, God's son, was so that others might receive sonship."[32]

30. The authorship of Ephesians is contested (see, e.g., Mitton, *Epistle to the Ephesians*); however, I will refer to its author as Paul for the sake of convenience, for the authorship of Ephesians is basically inconsequential for our purposes.

31. Heim (*Adoption*, 249) writes, "the involvement of the whole Trinity . . . bring[s] the believer into the intimate relationship of sonship."

32. Peppard, "Adopted and Begotten," 98.

5.3.2 Jesus Messiah

The redemption necessary to adopt children for God came at the expense of Jesus' perfect life. Again, Ephesians 1 professes: "God destined us to be his adopted children through Jesus Christ . . . We have been ransomed through his Son's blood, and we have forgiveness for our failures based on his overflowing grace, which he poured over us . . . " (Eph 1:5, 7–8, CEB; cf. Gal 4:5). Thus, Jesus' atoning and salvific death was the payment for adoption (or the ransom for redemption).

Utilizing another image within this adoption metaphorical framework, the apostle Paul likens the Mosaic Law, the Sinaitic Covenant as serving in the role of a foster parent or guardian, while it is Jesus who is Israel's—and all humanity's—True Parent. Before the *adoption* reference in Galatians 4:5 (see previous section), Paul develops his argument this way.

> Before faith came, we were guarded under the Law, locked up until faith that was coming would be revealed, so that the Law became our custodian until Christ so that we might be made righteous by faith. But now that faith has come, we are no longer under a custodian. You are all God's children through faith in Christ Jesus. All of you who were baptized into Christ have clothed yourselves with Christ. There is neither Jew nor Greek; there is neither slave nor free; nor is there male and female, for you are all one in Christ Jesus. Now if you belong to Christ, then indeed you are Abraham's descendants, heirs according to the promise. (Gal 3:23–29, CEB)

Indeed, liberation overtones not only color the fostering imagery of Galatians 3:23–39 but also brings vibrancy to the adoption metaphor in Galatians 4:1–7.[33] Accordingly, James Scott posits Galatians 4:1–2 is the type—"Israel's redemption to divine adoptive sonship . . . [at] the Exodus from Egypt"—and Galatians 4:3–7 is the antitype—"believer' redemption to divine adoptive

33. Cf. Peppard, "Adopted and Begotten," 95–96.

sonship . . . [at] the Second Exodus."[34] The second exodus is Jesus' offer of salvation—for people to come out of, to be liberated from the bondage of sin—which Jesus achieved upon his crucifixion and resurrection;[35] further, with the resurrection and ascension of Jesus the Christ, the new covenant and the kingdom of God are both inaugurated.

5.3.3 Holy Spirit

The adopted children of God (Eph 1:4–5), then, are those redeemed by the Son of God (Eph 1:7–8); and, the regenerative work of the Holy Spirit in the act and process of divine adoption, consequently, is the Holy Spirit's sealing of the new creation in Christ as a promissory note (Eph 1:13–14; cf. also 2 Cor 1:22; 5:5). Indeed, the indwelling presence of the Holy Spirit is the sign and foretaste of the reality of the divine adoption that has transacted. Paul elaborates:

> All who are led by God's Spirit are God's sons and daughters. You didn't receive a spirit of slavery to lead you back again into fear, but you received a Spirit that shows you are adopted as his children. With this Spirit, we cry, 'Abba, Father.' The same Spirit agrees with our spirit, that we are God's children. But if we are children, we are also heirs. We are God's heirs and fellow heirs with Christ, if we really suffer with him so that we can also be glorified with him. (Rom 8:14–17, CEB; cf. Gal 4:6–7)

Of course, calling God *Abba* is how Jesus himself addresses his Divine Parent when praying in the garden of Gethsemane (Mark 14:36).[36] Evidently, the ability to call God "daddy" (*Abba*) is evidence of regeneration, being born anew into the family of God as a child of God.[37] "As James Dunn notes, the Spirit dwelling in us

34. Scott, *Adoption*, 186.

35. In Luke 9:31 it states that Jesus knew he had to go to Jerusalem for his departure (Gk. *exodos*).

36. See further, Longenecker, "Metaphor of Adoption," 74.

37. Cf. Grassi, "Abba, Father (Mark 14:36)," 449–58.

is the spirit of adoption . . . precisely because it is 'the Spirit of his Son' (Gal 4:6; Rom 8:9–10) and links believers to Jesus, making us fellow children and heirs of God."[38]

Later, in the same discourse, Paul says, "We ourselves who have the Spirit . . . groan inside as we wait to be adopted and for our bodies to be set free" (Rom 8:23, CEB; cf. Rom 9:4). Romans 8 employs both the present and future tense,[39] which is indicative of the already/not-yet present nature of the kingdom of God in the overlapping of the ages (i.e., the age that is and the age to come).[40] To make sense of the present and future tense in Romans 8, as well as to highlight the Trinitarian activity in divine adoption, the following integrative illustration is propounded.[41]

An Integrated Illustration

In international adoption procedures for the United States there are two trips required of the parents when adopting a child abroad; in the first, the child is selected and paperwork and payments are made, and, in the second, more paperwork and payments are made whereupon the child makes the return trip with his/her new parents.[42] This general framework is analogous to God's adoption process and sheds light on the both the role of the Holy Spirit and Jesus' two advents.

In commencing the divine adoption plan, God sent Jesus to the world to (s)elect orphans to be adopted (i.e., all who come to faith in Christ). Upon his first trip, Jesus pays the adoption fees in full by sacrificing his perfect, righteous life; Jesus also completes all paperwork for adoption, putting into effect new documentation (the new covenant) for the children's new life. When Jesus makes

38. Johnson, "Waiting for Adoption," 310.

39. Scott, *Adoption*, 265; Burke, *Adopted*, 177–93; Peppard, "Adopted and Begotten," 96–97.

40. See Ladd, *Gospel of the Kingdom*.

41. Cf. also Platt, *Follow Me*, 25–29; Johnson, "Waiting for Adoption," 311.

42. See "Hague Visa Process."

his return, he will usher all adoptive (saved) children into the new heaven and new earth, the eternal home of the righteous (1 Pet 3).

In the interim period, between Jesus' first advent and second coming, the Holy Spirit is the seal on the legal adoption documentation, the guarantor that the adoptive act is both in process (sanctification) and complete (justification). In addition, the Holy Spirit is like the cell phone in that, until Jesus makes his second journey to Earth (glorification), direct communication can be experienced between the adopted children and their Divine Parent (cf. John 14:26; 1 Cor 2:11–12).

5.4 Legal Rights of Adopted Children

Once children are adopted, they experience a new existence; their identity, rights and responsibilities, as well as the benefits of being a legal, legitimate family member, are a novel reality. To shed light on the biblical epistolary engagement of these subsidiary issues of adoption, it is helpful to look at the background of adoptive practices in the Roman Empire.[43] Everett Ferguson states,

> Adoption was far more frequent and important in Roman society than it is today. The person adopted (at any age) was taken out of his previous condition, all old debts were cancelled, and he started a new life in the relation of sonship to the new *paterfamilias*, whose family name he took and to whose inheritance he was entitled. The new father now owned the adoptee's property, controlled his personal relationships, and had the right to disciple, while assuming responsibility for his support and liability for his actions—all just as with natural children born into the home. Adoption was a legal act, attested by witnesses.[44]

43. Lewis (*Spirit of Adoption*, 195) observes: "When Paul uses the metaphor of adoption, he is appropriating a piece of the Roman Imperial narrative that connects religious, political, and social realities to the advent of the Spirit as a result of the resurrection of Jesus."

44. Ferguson, *Backgrounds*, 65–66.

In the biblical appropriation of the adoption metaphor, many of these points are relevant. In particular, the right to inherit indicates that the adopted child is an heir.[45] In his epistles, Paul likewise maintains that those who receive Jesus' salvation are heirs of God (Gal 3:29; 4:7; Eph 3:6; Titus 3:7) and co-heirs with Christ (Rom 8:17). That which is inherited as adoptive children of God is also advanced in the New Testament, and it stands in contradistinction from both what was inherited and who inherited in Israelite society, as represented in the Old Testament.

5.4.1 Inheritance in the Old Testament

In the Old Testament, male children were typically the only demographic who could inherit land and assets from their family, from his father. There are two deviations from this norm, notwithstanding, and both are found in the context of the land apportionment after the Israelites' conquest of Canaan. First, sons who do not inherit are the Levites; while the other tribes of Israel all received territory, the priestly clan could only occupy cities within the twelve tribes of their kindred (Num 35:1–8; Josh 21). God explicates that the inheritance of the Levites is God's own self (Num 18:20; Deut 10:9; 18:1–2; Josh 13:14, 33; 14:3; Sir 45:20–22). Indeed, their ministry in the tabernacle/temple, in proximity to the presence of the LORD—a thing not allowed for any other tribesmen—was uniquely allotted to the descendants of Levi.[46]

A second exception to the typical standard of inheritance in the Old Testament is a case where daughters receive land. Zelophehad is said to have died with no sons, yet he did have five daughters (Num 27:1–11; 36:1–13).[47] These daughters of Zelophehad—Mahlah, Noah, Hoglah, Milcah, and Tirzah—request land inheritance of Moses so that the name of their father might not

45. Cf. Melnyk, "When Israel Was a Child," 253–55.

46. The tribe of Levi constituted a few families (Gershon, Kohath, and Merari [Gen 46:11; Exod 6:16]) who were together responsible for the priestly service (Num 3–4), along with the sons of Aaron, the priests (cf. Lev 1–9).

47. Cf. also Caleb's daughter in Joshua 15:13–19 and Judges 1:12–15.

perish from the memory/record of Israel. God does grant this request, even securing it to them in the event of their forthcoming marriages, and the daughters of Zelophehad remind Joshua of the same when land is being apportioned (Josh 17:1–13).[48]

5.4.2 Inheritance in the New Testament

In contrast to the near uniform standard of only males receiving inheritance in the Old Testament, the New Testament advances something much more equitable. In Christ, furthermore, not only are the recipients but also the contents of inheritance more expansive. The recipients of Christ's inheritance are all those who are saved by grace through faith in Christ alone and thereby are the new covenant people, the church, the bride of Christ; this means every Jew or gentile, slave or free, male or female, etc. who is in salvation-relationship with Jesus are children of God and heirs with Christ (cf. Gal 3:26–29).[49]

The inheritance of adoptive sons and daughters of God, then, is multifaceted and variegated. In addition to salvation (Heb 1:14; cf. Eph 1:11, 13–14, 18; Col 1:12), what is inherited in redemption in Christ is eternal life (Matt 19:29; Mark 10:17; Luke 10:25; 18:18) and the kingdom of God (Matt 5:5, 9; 25:34; cf. Rom 4:13; 1 Cor 6:9–10; 15:50; Eph 5:5 Gal 5:21). Relatedly, similar to the Levites' inheritance being God's own self, so do the saved in Christ receive the Triune God (cf. 5.3), as they minister in Christ (cf. 2 Cor 5:18; Eph 4:12); also, analogous to the other tribes of Israel receiving plots of land as an inheritance, the redeemed children of God will receive the new heavens and new earth as the home of the righteous (2 Pet 3:13; cf. Isa 65:17; 66:22; Rev 21:1).[50]

It is enlightening, moreover, to consider the precise time when an inheritance is received in the new covenant reality, i.e., when inheritance is conferred from one party to another.

48. See Russaw, *Daughters*, 14–17, 84–87, 143–46; Stiebert, *Fathers and Daughters*, 64–66.

49. Cf. Besançon Spencer, "Father-Ruler," 441.

50. See further, Walters, "Paul, Adoption, and Inheritance," 42–76.

Naturally, an inheritance is transferred to the child and heir upon the death of the *paterfamilias*; and the same is true in the New Testament/Covenant. It is upon the death of Jesus where many children are brought into glory, into an eternal inheritance (Heb 2:10; 9:15). Even still, because of Jesus' resurrection from the dead all the privileges and responsibilities of inheritance are enjoyed by the beneficiaries with the benefactor being alive and relationally engaged (Luke 15:11–32)![51] Peter articulates this well:

> Blessed be the God and Father of our Lord Jesus Christ! By his great mercy he has given us a new birth into a living hope through the resurrection of Jesus Christ from the dead, and into an inheritance that is imperishable, undefiled, and unfading, kept in heaven for you, who are being protected by the power of God through faith for a salvation ready to be revealed in the last time. (1 Pet 1:3–5, NRSV)

Because Jesus is a living Savior and the Christian's living hope, therefore, participating in Christ's inheritance is like being governed by a living will, for the Holy Spirit indwelling the disciple of Christ is the pledge of God's bequeathed salvation-life—in all its full array—for adopted children of God (Eph 1:13–14; 2 Cor 1:22; 5:5).

5.5 Children of God

With such a thoroughgoing adoption process and the grand scale of rights and inheritance, one's identity in Christ by the Spirit as a child of God is often reiterated in the New Testament. Like the phrase *born of God* (see chapter 2, 2.2.3), the phrase *children of God* is also frequently attested in the Johannine literature (John 1:12; 11:52; 1 John 3:1, 10; 5:2) to describe the beautifully wondrous reality of this divine familial relationship. In Romans 8–9, where over half the *adoption* verses occur, there is, in conjunction, the attestation of those adopted being legitimate *children of*

51. Cf. Kirk, "Appointed Son(s)," 242.

God (Rom 8:14, 16, 19, 21; 9:8; see also Gal 3:26; Phil 2:15). Jesus himself widens the progeny of the divine family in his Sermon on the Mount: "'Blessed are the peacemakers, for they will be called children of God'" (Matt 5:9, NRSV; cf. also Luke 20:36).

In all the New Testament occurrences of *children of God* (e.g., in the NRSV), there is linguistic variation in the original language. Whereas every Johannine instance features Gk. *teknon*, which is gender neutral and therefore is inclusive of female and male, only about half of the Pauline uses attest the same (Rom 8:16, 21; 9:8; Phil 2:15). In the remaining Pauline occurrences (Rom 8:14, 19; Gal 3:26), along with Jesus' teachings in the Gospels (Matt 5:9; Luke 20:36), the text technically reads *sons* (Gk. *huioi*) of God; nevertheless, though sonship is appropriated to accentuate traditional notions of inheritance (cf. 5.4.1),[52] the inclusion of the females/daughters demographic is surely intended.[53]

In a rare case, in the New Testament, both sons (Gk. *huios*) and daughters (Gk. *thugateras*) are specifically highlighted together. Concluding several consecutive Old Testament quotations, 2 Corinthians 6:18 (NRSV) reads, "I will be your father, and you shall be my sons and daughters, says the Lord Almighty."[54] It is generally believed this citation comes from 2 Samuel 7:14,[55] which is poignant for a few reasons. First, the source material cited only actually says "'I will be a father to him, and he shall be a son to me'" (2 Sam 7:14, NRSV); thus, the paraphrase expands the recipient from male to male and female and from singular to plural. Second,

52. Also, in the context of the beatitudes, Jesus avows: "'Blessed are the meek, for they will inherit the earth'" (Matt 5:5, NRSV).

53. E.g., while Galatians 3:26 reads "sons" (Gk. *huioi*) of God, the verses immediately following amplify: "As many of you as were baptized into Christ have clothed yourselves with Christ. There is no longer Jew or Greek, there is no longer slave or free, there is no longer male and female; for all of you are one in Christ Jesus. And if you belong to Christ, then you are Abraham's offspring, heirs according to the promise" (Gal 3:27–29, NRSV).

54. The only other New Testament occurrence of *sons* and *daughters* (of God) is Acts 2:17, which is an exact quotation from Joel 2:28. See further, Martens, "People of God," 225–53.

55. See e.g., USB4, 890.

2 Samuel 7:14 is God's adoption formula in instituting a king(ly dynasty); consequently, adoptive sons and daughters are "seated . . . with [God] in the heavenly places in Christ Jesus," the King of kings, as royalty (Eph 2:6, NRSV; cf. Rev 1:5). Such is the splendor and privilege of being (adoptive/saved) sons and daughters of God Almighty in Christ Jesus by the power of the Holy Spirit!

To sum up: Although there is slight analog in the Old Testament, the notion of adoption—specifically spiritual adoption on behalf of the Deity—is fully developed christologically in the New Testament as one (of many) metaphor(s) to illustrate redemption, salvation, and the divine trinitarian rescue mission (Rom 8–9; Gal 3–4; Eph 1). Sons and daughters both are adopted by the initiating love and plan of God, the adoption price vicariously through faith in Jesus Christ is paid, and the legal documentation and authorization is sealed by the Holy Spirit; in other words, God in kindness leads people to repentance (Rom 2:4; Titus 3:4) whereupon grace by faith in Christ Jesus saves a person (Rom 11:5–6; Eph 2:8–9); they are regenerated to new life—abundant and eternal (John 10:10b; 3:16)—by the empowering and sanctifying work of the Holy Spirit (Rom 9:11; 1 Cor 6:11). These gifts and more are the inheritance of adoptive children of God, who are legal and rightful heirs in Christ.

What does it look like for an adopted child of God to live within the household or family of God? What is the nature and process of growing and maturing into the likeness of the divine *paterfamilias* (viz., Christlikeness)? This complex set of issues are addressed in the next chapter.

6

Parenting as Discipleship

In this chapter, the life of the adopted children of God within the household or family of God is developed. Discipleship—both in Judaism and Christianity—is portrayed in metaphorical terms as parenting. Indeed, inculcation is akin to both parenting children and making disciples, the former being an analog for the latter; and, this holistic rearing and training—in the law of the LORD and the way of Christ Jesus by the Holy Spirit—of both biological and spiritual children is attested throughout Scripture.

To proceed methodically in this metaphorical topic, socio-religious inculcation within the family household/structure is briefly examined first in the Old and then in the New Testament. The biblical language dovetails into metaphoric depictions of the family of God, comprised of brothers and sisters of all ages sharing equal standing before the Divine Parent (Triune God) and their true elder brother (Jesus); alternatively, the metaphor alters to denote the role and need for spiritual parents (vs. spiritual baby-sitters) also. Mature and grown disciples of Christ are therefore mentors and role models for immature, yet developing, disciples of Christ to imitate and emulate; indeed, maturity of disciples in the household of God is God's intended design for the children of God, as they interact and engage with the world.

6.1 Parenting/Discipling in the Old Testament

Didacticism conspicuously surfaces in a few Old Testament texts. The teaching–learning semiotic relationship involves the parents' loving inculcation of their children and the honor incumbent upon the children unto their parents (Exod 20:12; Deut 5:16). The prosperous byproduct thereof is God's promise of a long, flourishing life in the promised land (Eph 6:2–3); thus, it is to this end that the Old Testament passages concerning inculcation instruct (cf. Deut 30:19–20).

Religious instruction within the household, and throughout Israelite society, is present initially in the annual Festival of Passover. Exodus 12–13 simultaneously legislates the ritual adherence of Passover and inculcates salvation history, as presented in the biblical narrative (cf. chapter 3, 3.1.1). The teachable moments are catalyzed upon the children's curiosity and inquiry.

> You should observe this ritual as a regulation for all time for you and your children. When you enter the land that the LORD has promised to give you, be sure that you observe this ritual. And when your children ask you, 'What does this ritual mean to you?' you will say, 'It is the Passover sacrifice to the LORD, for the LORD passed over the houses of the Israelites in Egypt. When he struck down the Egyptians, he spared our houses.' (Exod 12:24–27, CEB)

In another instance, Joshua orders a pillar monument of twelve stones to be erected once the Israelites had crossed the Jordan River. The purpose of this object was to serve as a mechanism, upon the occasion of children asking the meaning of the pillar, to testify to how God dried up the river before the ark of the covenant (Josh 4:6–7, 21–22). This retelling also serves to transmit the oral tradition of God's miraculous deliverance to the next (and, ideally, every subsequent) generation.

The most explicit, detailed, and methodical example in the Old Testament of religious inculcation, though, is the *Shema* (Deut 6:4–9; 11:18–21), which is also considered the greatest commandment (Matt 22:36–39; Mark 12:28–31). *Šəma‘* is Heb. for *hear* or *listen*; and it connotes the expectation of obedience, adherence.[1] Thus, for the covenant people of God the following directives are parental and communal measures for raising their children in the fear and knowledge of YHWH God.

> Hear, O Israel: The LORD is our God, the LORD alone. You shall love the LORD your God with all your heart, and with all your soul, and with all your might. Keep these words that I am commanding you today in your heart. Recite them to your children and talk about them when you are at home and when you are away, when you lie down and when you rise. Bind them as a sign on your hand, fix them as an emblem on your forehead, and write them on the doorposts of your house and on your gates. (Deut 6:4–9, NRSV; cf. Exod 13:9; Prov 6:20–23)

In distinction from the prior examples where the impetus for inculcation was the child's occasional inquisitiveness, here the inculcation is mandated to be regularly initiated by the parents. There are several meaningful pedagogical aspects of the *Shema* which deserve elaboration.

First, the love for God is described in thoroughly holistic language: to love God with one's entire heart, soul, and strength.[2] The heart was conceived as the seat of intellect, and the soul the place of emotion;[3] "might" or "strength" (NIV) is Heb. *mə'ōd* and indicates *excess*[4]—viz., if there is anything else with which to love God beyond a person's heart and soul, then one should love God with what might still remain. It is rare to have such compounded,

1. *HALOT* 2:1570–74; BDB 1033–34.

2. Jesus adds *mind* when he cites the *Shema* (Matt 22:37; Mark 12:30; cf. Luke 10:27). This mental faculty should not be understood as a fourth, separate element; rather, Greek philosophy (at home in Roman society) distinguished between mind and heart, whereas Eastern/Hebrew thought saw these as one and the same. Consequently, Jesus is contextualizing the *Shema* for his audience. See further, McKnight, *Jesus Creed.*

3. *HALOT* 1:513–15; BDB 523–25. Cf. Smith, "Heart and Innards," 427–36.

4. BDB 547; cf. *HALOT* 1:538–39.

superlative syntax in Hebrew prose, for any one of these faculties conveys a fully devoted loyalty; consequently, much emphasis and weight is placed on this central and greatest command of loving the One God.

Second, love for God is to be cultivated and expressed personally, privately, and publicly. This loving emanation ranges from the individual's heart and soul (vv. 5–6), to the family's home (vv. 7, 9), to the wider society (vv. 7–8). Faithfulness and devotion to God is envisioned, therefore, to permeate a culture. Relatedly, since there will always be children born and parents to teach them the way of the LORD, the *Shema* also indicates the love of/for God is to be generational.

Third, the inculcation of the premier command of love for God is to be taught in a pedagogically integrative manner—viz., through the learning means of auditory, visual, tactile, and kinesthetic. Parents are to impress upon children loyalty to YHWH through orally reciting instruction and conversing about the command's meaning (v. 7). The greatest commandment is visually engaged when beholding phylacteries bound upon the hands and foreheads of the men of the community (v. 8).[5] When the *Shema* was written on gates and doorposts, this was a tactile means of remembering the foremost significant command from God (v. 9). The kinesthetic aspects can be found in the walking activity, even lying down and rising (v. 7); when these movements are linked to dialogue regarding dedication to God, the doctrine becomes more integrated into one's being.[6]

5. *Phylacteries* (cf. Matt 23:5) were essentially boxes with scriptures enclosed inside; and these were tied with leather bands, strapped around wrists, as bracelets, and foreheads, as frontlets. The most common scriptures in phylacteries, usually written on fragments of parchment, was the Aaronic blessing (Num 6:24–26). See further Smoak, *Priestly Blessing*.

6. Cf. Suzuki, "Brain-Changing Benefits."

6.2 Parenting/Discipling in the New Testament

The parental and societal inculcation in the way of the LORD continues far beyond the canonization of the Hebrew Bible, even to the present day. Before approaching the New Testament, Philo of Alexandria, a Jewish philosopher and contemporary of Jesus, affirms this educational way of life of the Jews in the first century CE. He writes, "Jews . . . had been taught in a manner from their very swaddling-clothes by their parents, and teachers, and instructors, and even before that by their holy laws, and also by their unwritten maxims and customs, to believe that there was but one God, their Father and the Creator of the world."[7]

Therefore, when Paul in his letters refers to Timothy being raised by his mother and grandmother, this was surely in the inculcating tradition of Deuteronomy 6:4–9 and 11:18–21. Paul will use this familial religious upbringing, furthermore, to illustrate that discipleship in Christ is a similar rearing, nurturing, and guiding process in/for the church. Both the natural family and the supernatural family of God, consequently, are delineated in 1 and 2 Timothy.

Paul writes Timothy:

> I am reminded of your sincere faith, a faith that lived first in your grandmother Lois and your mother Eunice and now, I am sure, lives in you. For this reason I remind you to rekindle the gift of God that is within you through the laying on of my hands; for God did not give us a spirit of cowardice, but rather a spirit of power and of love and of self-discipline. (2 Tim 1:5–7, NRSV)

Timothy's natural father is not mentioned because he was a Greek (cf. Acts 16:1); potentially not sharing the same convictions of Judaism, he did not participate in the religious inculcation of Timothy. Nevertheless, Timothy's mother and grandmother were godly women, committed to his religious upbringing (cf. Prov 22:6). Paul likewise maintains that he had a hand in Timothy's maturing in faith, since he imparted the Holy Spirit to Timothy;

7. Philo, *Gig.* 1:115.

consequently, Paul sees himself as Timothy's spiritual father (see further in next section).

In light of God's plan revealed in the life and work of Jesus, Paul encourages ongoing growth in knowledge in the Scripture, christologically, exhorting,

> continue in what you have learned and firmly believed, knowing from whom you learned it, and how from childhood you have known the sacred writings that are able to instruct you for salvation through faith in Christ Jesus. All scripture is inspired by God and is useful for teaching, for reproof, for correction, and for training in righteousness, so that everyone who belongs to God may be proficient, equipped for every good work. (2 Tim 3:14–17, NRSV)

In addition to his parents in the faith (2 Tim 1:5–7), Timothy has also been weaned and reared on Scripture from birth (Gk. *brephos*) throughout his childhood (2 Tim 3:15a). "Scripture" (Gk. *grapha*) is referred to here as the sacred writings (Gk. *hieros grammata*),[8] which is the Hebrew Bible, the Old Testament.[9] Furthermore, the Scripture is effective for discipleship in Jesus, Israel's Messiah/Christ and the world's Savior.

Discipleship in Christ is, significantly, cast in verbiage of filial inculcation. Teaching (Gk. *didaskalia*) and training (Gk. *paideia*), in particular, are those guiding and shaping actions typically associated with parenting (cf. Prov 1:7–8; 3:11–12; 4:1–2).[10] Also, Gk. *paideia* may alternatively be translated "discipline";[11] utilized in

8. From this compound term (*hieros grammata*) we get the word *hagiography*, holy writings.

9. Eventually the New Testament—as the fulfillment appendix of the Hebrew Bible—is deemed inspired Scripture. See, e.g., Metzger, *Canon of the New Testament*.

10. These two Gk. terms are employed together in Sirach 39:8. Also, similarly, training (Gk. *paideia*) and teaching (Gk. *mesmos*) occurs in synonymous parallelism—and in a parenting context—in Proverbs 1:8 LXX. For the absence of these measure unto the opposite result, see Proverbs 5:12–13.

11. BDAG, 748–49.

parenting contexts (Eph 6:4; Heb 12:5, 7–8, 11), discipline is that impulsion indicative of God as Divine Parent too (chapter 1, 1.4).

6.3 Disciple-maker as Parent, Disciple as Child, and Fellow Disciples as Siblings

Throughout his letters about the church of Jesus, Paul instructs and admonishes that Christian relationships are to be like those of family members, for the community of the redeemed and reconciled is the family of God (cf. 1 Tim 3:15; see 6.6). Specifically, Paul advises Timothy that ecclesial relationships are to be like those of spiritual siblings: "Do not speak harshly to an older man, but speak to him as to a father, to younger men as brothers, to older women as mothers, to younger women as sisters—with absolute purity" (1 Tim 5:1–2, NRSV). Here Paul is elaborating on the same teaching of Jesus, when the latter said that all who do the will of God are Jesus' (mother and) brothers and sisters (Matt 12:46–50; Mark 3:31–35; Luke 8:19–21).

In addition to all disciples of Jesus being understood as siblings in Christ, another familial dimension is introduced in the New Testament: disciple-makers and those being discipled partake in a parent–child relationship in the Spirit. Paul employs this metaphorical language commonly to refer to his spiritual sons; for example:

- To Timothy, my true child in the faith. (1 Tim 1:2, CEB; cf. also 2 Tim 1:2; Phil 2:22)
- To Titus, my true child in a common faith. (Titus 1:4, CEB)
- As you know, we dealt with each one of you like a father with his children, urging and encouraging you and pleading that you lead a life worthy of God, who calls you into his own kingdom and glory. (1 Thess 2:11–12, NRSV)

It is noteworthy that the two spiritual sons of Paul, explicitly mentioned by name as such, each receive one or more epistles from their spiritual father. Furthermore, it is precisely in 1 Timothy and

Titus where Paul adjures his spiritual children with the task of appointing and establishing elders (and deacons)—and the role of church leadership is markedly colored in familial tones of spiritual parents, or mentors, who are commissioned to mature disciples of Jesus in the body of Christ (1 Tim 3:14–15).[12] Those to-be appointed elders (spiritual parents) are, in turn, to disciple (parent in the faith) other less mature followers of Christ.

6.4 (The Need for) Spiritual Parents vs. Spiritual Guardians

The absence of spiritual parents, inversely, is detrimental to the body of Christ, the family of God. In contrast to spiritual children having good, effective spiritual parents, Paul, in another context, contrasts the role and influence of a spiritual parent versus that of a spiritual guardian. To the church in Corinth, the apostle conveys,

> I am . . . writing this . . . to admonish you as my beloved children. For though you might have ten thousand guardians in Christ, you do not have many fathers. Indeed, in Christ Jesus I became your father through the gospel. I appeal to you, then, be imitators of me. For this reason I sent you Timothy, who is my beloved and faithful child in the Lord, to remind you of my ways in Christ Jesus, as I teach them everywhere in every church. (1 Cor 4:14–17, NRSV)

Paul's paternal rite and role for the Jesus-disciples in Greece is variously described. Conversion to faith in Christ, or salvation, is metaphorically rendered in birthing language—Paul begat (Gk. *gennaō*) or "gave birth to" them (CEB). Being a (spiritual) father is superior to being a (spiritual) guardian unto (spiritual) children, i.e., those young and immature in Christ. The term *guardian* (Gk. *paidagōgos*) means a trainer of boys, i.e., *a tutor*;[13] and it is the

12. Verner, *Household of God*; cf. also Cole, *Primal Fire*, 38–50.

13. BDAG, 748. "The term *paidagogos* (v. 15) refers not so much to a 'teacher' as to a 'guardian' (cf. Gal. 3:24), the servant who walked a rich child to school and back home and helped him with his recitations at home and so was

derivative of our word *pedagogy*: "the art, science, or profession of teaching; especially: education."[14]

The distinction between father and guardian is significant. Philo of Alexandria records a pledge that Roman Emperor Gaius made to his cousin, Tiberius Gemellus, that resembles both adoption formula and the responsibility of tutelage.[15] "'I, therefore,' said he: 'passing over and being superior to all tutors [Gk. *paidagōgous*], and masters [Gk. *didaskalous*], and guardians [Gk. *epitropous*], register myself as his father, and him as my son.'"[16] Though this is a fabrication on the part of the emperor and does not transpire, the distinction between guardian and father is nonetheless clear, and is likewise what Paul delineates in 1 Corinthians 4:15.[17]

Parentage exceeds guardianship in that, while guardianship is supplementary for a person's childhood development, a parent is someone a child can emulate throughout the whole of life (cf. chapter 1, 1.5).[18] Paul sends Timothy to the Corinthians, because, as Paul's image and likeness in Christ, as Paul's true son in Christ (6.2, 6.3), he will be an example for the juvenile Jesus-disciples to follow the same pattern in growing into the fullness of Christ, just as Timothy has by following Paul's example.[19] Thus, to be discipled

---

also a tutor to some degree. Paul's use of this word may be a reference to the many local 'sages' of the *ekklēsia* in Corinth, rather than Apollos, whom Paul classes with himself" (Witherington, *Conflict and Community*, 147).

14. C.v. "Pedagogy," https://www.merriam-webster.com/dictionary/pedagogy.

15. Besançon Spencer, "Father-Ruler," 441.

16. Philo, *Gig.* 1:27b; cf. Philo, *Mut.* 1:217; Philo, *Her.* 1:295.

17. "That Paul should have so ended his lengthy discussion in 1 Cor. 1:10–4:21 with the father image of justice or moderation suggests that he is invoking an authoritative relationship over the congregation as its founding father, the impact of which is more readily appreciated when placed against the background of its imperial use in this Roman colony during the Claudian Principate" (Lassen, "Father Image," 136).

18. Cf. Lockwood, "Spiritual Fatherhood," 81–127.

19. Goodrich (*Paul As an Administrator of God*, 146) synopsizes: "The Corinthian believers, as Paul's own work in the Lord and the seal of his apostleship (1 Cor 9.1–2), are nothing less than Paul's spiritual children (4.14–16). As such, Paul possesses the right to admonish and instruct them to imitate him as

in the faith is the emulate one's spiritual parent (disciple-maker) to the extent that one becomes just as that parent, and then, in turn, spiritually parents (disciples) others.[20] Each disciple-maker must clearly exhibit Jesus and parent disciples into Christ, moreover, not themselves (cf. 1 Cor 1:10–17; 3:5–17); as a result, Paul exhorts, "be imitators of God, as beloved children" of God (Eph 5:1, NRSV).

6.5 Maturity: God's Goal for God's Children

The goal that God has for the children of God is to grow, mature, and, as (spiritual) adults, accurately resemble their Divine Parent to the family of faith and to the world (cf. chapter 3). In Ephesians 4, Paul utilizes a few illustrations in encouraging the growth and maturation of the body of Christ; one positive analogy is architectural (v. 16bβ), and one negative analogy nautical (v. 14). However, the predominant analogy to speak to both maturity (vv. 13b, 16b) and immaturity (vv. 14aα, 15) in Christ Jesus is an anthropological one.

> God's goal is for us to become mature adults—to be fully grown, measured by the standard of the fullness of Christ. As a result, we aren't supposed to be infants any longer who can be tossed and blown around by every wind that comes from teaching with deceitful scheming and the tricks people play to deliberately mislead others. Instead, by speaking the truth with love, let's grow in every way into Christ, who is the head. The whole body grows from him, as it is joined and held together by all the supporting ligaments. The body makes itself grow in that it builds itself up with love as each one does their part. (Eph 4:13b–16, CEB)

---

he imitates Christ (4.16; 11.1)."

20. Wilkins, "Imitate, Imitators," 3:392. Cf. Michaelis, "μιμέομαι κλη," 4:659–74.

What "maturity looks like [is] Jesus";[21] and what growing into maturity looks like is speaking the truth in love, or Gospel articulation. Baby-talk is cute when it comes from a toddler; but it is not so endearing should baby-talk come from an adult. "Paul . . . clarifies the truth that we are to speak to one another in verse 21 [of Eph 4]. He states, 'The truth is Jesus.' 'Speaking the truth in love,' for Paul, is shorthand for 'speaking what is true about Jesus' to one another—that is speaking the gospel to one another."[22] It is this maturity in Christ which ensures one is not swept away, or tossed to and fro, by false teaching (Eph 4:14), which consequently is a regression in discipleship.

One summer recently, my family and friends of ours vacationed in Charleston, SC; and a big part of our fun was swimming in the warm Atlantic Ocean. There was a section of the beach that was demarcated as a public park and staffed with several lifeguards. I was playing in the waves with my daughters (who were ages nine, seven, and six at the time), yet we had to relocate about every fifteen minutes due to the riptide. Wanting to stay within the safest area, I would routinely have us all hold hands and as I pulled my girls back into the park parameters. As a grown adult, I could give counter resistance and move against the current; however, the riptide kept sweeping my kids along as they were not able to resist the power of the waves. Figuratively, getting swept along by the riptide is what "teaching with deceitful scheming and the tricks people play to deliberately mislead others" is like; conversely, to be fully grown indicates the ability to withstand the cultural currents contrary to the way and teachings of Jesus and to steadfastly circumnavigate them in following Christ.

Jesus himself taught that the goal of his disciples is to become like himself: "A disciple is not above the teacher, but everyone who is fully qualified will be like the teacher" (Luke 6:40, NRSV; Matt 10:24-25a). Dietrich Bonhoeffer expounds, "It is only because [Jesus] became like us that we can become like him. It is only because we are identified with [Jesus] that we can become like him. By

21. Vanderstelt, *Gospel Fluency*, 28.

22. Vanderstelt, *Gospel Fluency*, 28.

being transformed into [Jesus'] image, we are enabled to model our lives on his."[23] Emulation and imitation is concomitant to discipleship, indeed.

6.6 Household of God

As biological families live together in the same household, so similarly does the family of God live together as the household of faith (cf. chapter 5, 5.2.2).[24] While metaphors often get mixed in biblical literature, there is coherence that the church (1 Tim 3:15), the new temple (1 Pet 2:5), and the eschatological sanctuary (Eph 2:19) are all parallel with the house(hold) (Gk. *oikeios/oikos*) of God (1 Pet 4:17). Furthermore, Jesus is the "great priest over the house [Gk. *oikos*] of God" (Heb 10:21, NRSV), "the family [Gk. *oikeios*] of faith" (Gal 6:10, NRSV). Such is the constitution of the eternal household and family of God.

In synopsizing the relational dynamics in the family of God (*deusfamilias*), Deborah Sawyer juxtaposes it with the cultural milieu of the New Testament world and accentuates how children of God must always have "[r]adical dependency on God the parent" (cf. John 15:1–8).[25]

> Paul uses familial concepts of birth and new life, and of parenting, both divine and with Paul as surrogate parent. Paul's new *deusfamilias*, a term we can adopt to accentuate the Roman context for Paul's activities and emerging theology, is a mimesis of the Roman paterfamilias—and within this new family believers remain children. As children, corporately symbolising their glorified 'sibling' Christ in one family, boundaries of class, race and gender may be abrogated, but as part of a familial body they remain under the control of the *deusfamilias*. This context allows us to see in a new light early Christian attitudes to

23. Bonhoeffer, *Cost of Discipleship*, 344.

24. See further Coloe, *Household of God*; Balch, "Paul, Families, and Households," 258–92.

25. Sawyer, *God, Gender and the Bible*, 124.

> male and female relations, martyrdom and the potential political threat of the emerging new religion of Christianity within the Roman Empire.[26]

In summary, the inculcation, particularly within the family unit, commanded by God and practiced by the Israelites serves as a foundational framework for discipleship in Christ within the family of God. The family of God, from a christological viewpoint, comprises of redeemed and regenerated, reconciled and restored males and females who, in the Spirit, are brothers and sisters in Christ. To grow in maturity—and yet to ever be childlike in faith and dependent upon God as Divine Parent—is God's design for God's saved, adopted children. The metaphor of the divine family also morphs to illustrate how disciple-makers are like spiritual parents of spiritual children, disciples; nonetheless, Jesus as the Savior and Son of God is understood as Christians' elder brother, and even (part of) the Divine Parent.

26. Sawyer, *God, Gender and the Bible*, 120.

Conclusion

In this culminative move, a summary of findings shall be relayed; this synopsis highlights each personage in and the main facets of the family of God, as examined throughout the breadth of the Bible. Subsequently, some implications shall be disclosed; a few aspects of orthopraxis (correct conduct) flowing from orthodoxy (correct doctrine) are suggested, which may be integrated into the fabric of life in Christ.

Summary

Initially (introduction), the figurative nexus of God as a Divine Parent and humankind as God's children was proffered in the paradigmatic text concerning how humanity is created in the image of God: Genesis 1:26–27. From that point of departure, God's plurality of singularity and the capacity to (pro)create is corollary of humankind. Consequently, God transcends gender (as an infinite Being) yet also condescends to reveal Godself by means of gender diversity, by virtue of the *imago Dei*; and this facilitates the occasion for humans to metaphorically view and understand God as a Divine Parent and humankind as God's child(ren).

God as Father (chapter 1) is one gendered metaphor to describe our Divine Parent. It was discovered that in only approximately a dozen Old Testament verses is God portrayed paternally; and, often *father* is appositional with other terms, such as *creator*. Most of the discussion cataloguing the characteristics of God's parenthood as a Father centered on the New Testament, which illustrated and elaborated upon the same character traits put forth in the Old Testament—namely, God is a good, gift-giving Father, a loving and just Father, and a merciful Father.

God as Mother (chapter 2) is another gendered metaphor to describe our Divine Parent. In the Bible, each member of the Godhead is depicted in feminine and maternal terms. Indeed, the typical characteristics reserved for mothers and motherhood are evidenced with God Almighty, Jesus Christ, and the Holy Spirit—specifically, language and imagery evoking birthing and amniotic fluid, the capacity for comfort (womb-likeness) and compassion.

Based on being a Divine Parent, God consequently has progeny; sometimes God's child is personified, in the Bible, as a son (chapter 3). Israel is God's firstborn child (Exod 4:22; Hos 11:1), who is called out of Egypt; at first Israel is a compliant child, yet later he becomes rebellious and disobedient. Eventually Jesus' advent means the incarnation of the Son of God; Jesus is the obedient child before his Heavenly Parent, thereby redeeming Israel's historic life (failure). Further, Jesus' sonship (or divine child-nature) becomes a communalized reality for his disciples.

God's progeny (Israel) is alternatively portrayed, in the Old Testament, as a daughter (chapter 4). Daughter Israel is depicted as an abandoned infant whom God saves and raises; she is well loved and provided for in her adolescence. In her adulthood, Israel's covenantal unfaithfulness is figuratively rendered as a licentious lifestyle (Ezek 16) which has disastrous results for Daughter Zion (Lamentations), as she is also known. Once, Jesus restored a woman whom he calls *daughter*; this seems to indicate that those who receive salvation are enfolded into God's family, as divine daughters (children).

While Israel is God's natural child, so to speak, God's compassion for orphans (and widows and immigrants) is so great that, in the New Testament (era), God adopts many more children (gentiles) into the family of God (chapter 5). Triune God's salvation is portrayed metaphorically as an adoption process and its pursuant familial relationship: God Almighty orchestrates the adoption plan, Jesus Christ pays the adoption price with his life, and the Holy Spirit's indwelling presence in adopted (regenerated) children of God is the deposit ensuring the adoption. Furthermore, whereas typically only males could inherit corporeal items in ancient Israelite culture, God's new covenant adopted sons and daughters inherit eternal life and the kingdom of God, and more; thus, gender equity is realized in Christ Jesus (Gal 3:27–28).

Parenting, as perceived in both the Old and New Testaments, in the context of a family—and community—of faith, is seen as discipleship (chapter 6); and discipleship is painted in terms of spiritual parenting (Deut 6:4–9; 2 Tim 1:5–7; 3:14–17). As the family of God metaphor augments in the new covenant/church era, disciple-makers of Christ are as parents and those being discipled into Christ are as children, and fellow disciples in Christ are as siblings one to another. Pauline exhortation for spiritual parents over against spiritual guardians is formative (1 Cor 4:14–17). Ultimately, God's goal for God's children is maturity to the extent that disciples of Jesus grow up into Christ (Eph 4) and emulate their Divine Parent.

Implications

The implications of the biblical theology of the family of God are perhaps innumerable. A general schema by which to integrate biblical truth into personal lives on this topic may well be this: "be imitators of God, as beloved children" (Eph 5:1, NRSV). Following the ordering of the preceding chapters, a selection of specific implications of the unfolding acts of our Divine Parent is proffered.

When considering the parentage of God, it is noteworthy that despite being metaphorically portrayed in the Bible as both fatherly and motherly, (the Triune) God is *one* (Deut 6:4; cf. 1 John 5:5–8; John 17:21–23). Beyond a reference to *mono*theism, this implies that God is a single parent (figuratively). Today, families with single/solo parents make up approximately one-third of households in the United States;[27] the parenting experiences of these single/solo parents are often challenging and harrowing. That YHWH is scripturally rendered as a Divine, single (as it were) Parent is, consequently, potentially deeply meaningful for the single/solo parent, for God is especially compassionate toward the widow and orphan (and immigrant), which in today's terms may be analogous to the single/solo parent family—particularly if there is a lack of flourishing and oppression experienced by said family (cf. chapter 6).

It is significant that God's child is rendered in the Old Testament both in (metaphorical) terms of a son and a daughter. This ostensibly affirms the value and human dignity of both sexes/genders; thus, irrespective of the reader's gender identity, or whether the reader is experiencing gender confusion and/or dysphoria, there are attributes and characteristics within this gendered, child of God metaphor which are universal in pertaining to relationship with God. Furthermore, whether one is a transgender or an intersex person, for example, the reader may still readily relate as a child of God, for the Bible addresses all humanity and every personhood, beckoning them to be reconciled to God as adopted (saved) children of YHWH God in Christ Jesus by the Holy Spirit: note the nonbinary biblical terms like "new creation" in Christ (2 Cor 5:17; Gal 6:15, NRSV) and the "new humanity" wrought by Jesus (Eph 2:15, NRSV).

What is evident in the New Testament is that Jesus is the very child of God. Concerning the relationship between the Christ and YHWH, the Gospels show that God expresses approval of Jesus even before he performs kingdom ministry (Matt 3:16b–17) as well as throughout his kingdom ministry (Matt 17:5). The perfect life of Jesus Christ and the Father's approval of his child is significant, for this same divine favor is transmuted to the believer of Christ Jesus. Too often inordinate amounts of time and energy go into striving for the approval of a(n earthly) parent, which is often elusive and/or rarely forthcoming. However, the Jesus-disciple

27. See "Majority of Children Live with Two Parents"; Livingston, "About One-third of U.S. Children."

receives the Divine Parent's approval, favor, delight, etc. in Christ because of what Jesus has done to secure it on their behalf (cf. Heb 2:10; 4:14–16; 6:20)!

It is often espoused in culture that everyone—every single human being—is a child of God. The thinking is as follows: if God created humankind, then all humanity is a child of the Heavenly Parent (cf. introduction). This is both true in one sense and not true in another sense. As our investigation has shown, salvation in Jesus Christ is the reality for the *adopted* child of God. Perhaps all humans are children of God, yet there are those who are estranged (unregenerate) from their Divine Parent and those who are reconciled (regenerate) to their Divine Parent (cf. Luke 15:11–32). Therefore, to be children of God who belong to the Divine Parent salvifically and eternally is to be adopted in Christ Jesus by the Holy Spirit.

As a counterpart to spiritual adoption, imitating God as beloved children of God (Eph 5:1) includes and encompasses natural adoption (cf. chapter 5). For as it states in a deuterocanonical book: "Be like a parent to orphans, and take care of their mothers as for your own wife or husband. Do this, and you will be like a child of the Most High, and God will love you more than your own mother does." (Sir 4:10, CEB; cf. Job 31:18). Adoption, or foster-care for that matter, then, is not only a noble humanitarian enterprise, it may, additionally, be an undertaking catalyzed by spiritual conviction as an expression, an exhibition of the Gospel.

Discipleship is what maturing in the family of God and ministering from the family of God looks like for the redemptively adopted child of God. Therefore, it is imperative for each Christ-follower to be discipled and disciple others in Jesus (cf. 2 Tim 2:2; 1 Cor 11:1). Many Christians may actually be *job shadowing* Jesus their whole lives instead of being apprentices of Jesus. In the former instance, Christians show up, observe, learn, and even participate in Christian gatherings and functions; in the latter instance, Christian apprentices, as journeymen, are fully equipped to work in the family business: to articulate the gospel and enact gospel reality, so that more estranged children are adopted into the family of God, reconciled to the Divine Parent.

Hugh Halter illustrates:

> Biblical apprenticeship is about three things: (1) becoming like Jesus, (2) doing what Jesus did, and (3) doing the above with the types of people Jesus liked spending time with. . . . Here's how you can know if you are actually an apprentice: people respond to you like they did to Jesus. People are drawn to you. People seek you out for help. People like you, respect you, and want to live like you live. . . . the people of the world whom Jesus died for will want to be our friends. That's what an apprentice will experience.[28]

Finally, the family of God is a place of being, belonging, and becoming. Having undergone divine adoption (salvation in Christ Jesus), the individual's *being*, or identity, is a child of God. Once a regenerate and reconciled child of God, that individual has a vital sense of *belonging*—a home and a place in the family of God, complete with a present Divine Parent as well as siblings who have also experienced adoption in Christ Jesus (salvation). With one's identity and belonging secure, the redeemed child of God is enveloped in a conducive context to *become* like Jesus (cf. Matt 10:24-25a; Luke 6:40)—i.e., to "grow up in every way into him who is the head, into Christ" (Eph 4:15b, NRSV), or, in other words, "to be conformed to the image of [God's] Son" (Rom 8:29b, NRSV).

28. Halter, *Sacrilege*, 43, 44.

Bibliography

Aarde, Andries G. van. "The Carpenter's Son (Mt 13:55): Joseph and Jesus in the Gospel of Matthew and Other Texts." *Neotestamentica* 34 (2000) 173–90.

Albright, William F. "The Names SHADDAI and ABRAM." *Journal of Biblical Literature* 54 (1935) 173–204.

Alexander, T. Desmond, and Brian S. Rosner, eds. *New Dictionary of Biblical Theology*. Downers Grove, IL: InterVarsity, 2010.

Aristotle. *Politics*. Edited and translated by H. Rackham. Loeb Classical Library 264. Cambridge: Harvard University Press, 1967.

Balch, David L. "Paul, Families, and Households." In *Paul in the Greco-Roman World: A Handbook*, edited by J. Paul Sampley, 258–92. London: Trinity Press International, 2003.

Banks, Robert J. *Paul's Idea of Community: Spirit and Culture in Early House Churches*. 3rd ed. Grand Rapids: Baker Academic, 2020.

Bartlett, David L. "Adoption in the Bible." In *The Child in the Bible*, edited by Terence E. Fretheim and Beverly Roberts Gaventa, 375–98. Grand Rapids: Eerdmans, 2008.

Beale, Gregory K. "The Use of Hosea 11:1 in Matthew 2:15: One More Time." *Journal of the Evangelical Theological Society* 55 (2012) 697–715.

Bennett, William. "The Sons of the Father: The Fatherhood of God in the Synoptic Gospels." *Interpretation* 4 (1950) 12–23.

Besançon Spencer, Aída. "Father-Ruler: The Meaning of the Metaphor 'Father' for God in the Bible." *Journal of the Evangelical Theological Society* 39 (1996) 433–42.

Betsworth, Sharon, and Julie Faith Parker, eds. *T&T Clark Handbook of Children in the Bible and the Biblical World*. London: Bloomsbury Academic, 2019.

Bibb, Bryan. "There's No Sex in Your Violence: Patriarchal Translation in Ezekiel 16 and 23." *Review & Expositor* 111 (2014) 337–45.

Bird, Phyllis A. "'Male and Female He Created Them': Gen 1:27b in the Context of the Priestly Account of Creation." *Harvard Theological Review* 74 (1981) 129–59.

Bock, Darrell L. *Luke 1:1—9:50*. Baker Exegetical Commentary on the New Testament. Grand Rapids: Baker Academic, 1994.

Bonhoeffer, Dietrich. *The Cost of Discipleship*. Rev. ed. New York: Collier; MacMillian, 1963.

Brown, Jeannine K. "Is the Future of Biblical Theology Story-Shaped?" *Horizons in Biblical Theology* 37 (2015) 13–31.

Bruce, F. F. "Typology." In *IBD* 3:1602–3.

Brueggemann, Walter. "Vulnerable Children, Divine Passion, and Human Obligation." In *The Child in the Bible*, edited by Terence E. Fretheim and Beverly Roberts Gaventa, 399–422. Grand Rapids: Eerdmans, 2008.

Budin, Stephanie Lynn. "Reduced to Her Bare Essentials: Bronze Age Piriform Pendants in the Levant." *Near Eastern Archaeology* 79 (2016) 166–73.

Bullock, C. Hassell. "Ezekiel, Bridge between the Testaments." *Journal of the Evangelical Theological Society* 25 (1982) 23–31.

Burke, Trevor J. *Adopted into God's Family: Exploring a Pauline Metaphor*. New Studies in Biblical Theology 22. Downers Grove, IL: InterVarsity, 2006.

Childs, Brevard S. *Biblical Theology of the Old and New Testaments: Theological Reflection on the Christian Bible*. Minneapolis: Fortress, 1993.

———. *The Book of Exodus: A Critical, Theological Commentary*. Old Testament Library. Philadelphia: Westminster, 1974.

———. *Isaiah: A Commentary*. Old Testament Library. Louisville: Westminster John Knox, 2001.

———. *Old Testament Theology in a Canonical Context*. Philadelphia: Fortress, 1985.

Claassens, L. Juliana M. *Mourner, Mother, Midwife: Reimagining God's Delivering Presence in the Old Testament*. Louisville: Westminster John Knox, 2012.

———. "Transforming God-Language: The Metaphor of God as Abusive Spouse (Ezekiel 16) in Conversation with the Portrayal of God in *The Color Purple*." *Scriptura* 113 (2014) 1–11.

Cole, Neil. *Primal Fire: Reigniting the Church with the Five Gifts of Jesus*. Carol Stream, IL: Tyndale Momentum, 2014.

Coloe, Mary L. *Dwelling in the Household of God: Johannine Ecclesiology and Spirituality*. Collegeville, MN: Liturgical, 2007.

———. "Temple Imagery in John." *Interpretation* 63 (2009) 368–81.

Comer, John Mark. *God Has a Name*. Grand Rapids: Zondervan, 2017.

Conway, Mary L. "Daughter Zion: Metaphor and Dialogue in the Book of Lamentations." In *Daughter Zion: Her Portrait, Her Response*, edited by Mark J. Boda et al., 101–26. Ancient Israel and Its Literature 13. Atlanta: Society of Biblical Literature, 2012.

Crouch, Carly L. "Genesis 1:26-7 as a Statement of Humanity's Divine Parentage." *Journal of Theological Studies* 61 (2010) 1–15.

D'Angelo, Mary Rose. "Intimating Deity in the Gospel of John: Theological language and 'Father' in 'Prayers of Jesus.'" *Semeia* 85 (1999) 59–82.

Das, A. Andrew. "1 Corinthians 11:17–34 Revisited." *Concordia Theological Quarterly* 62 (1998) 187–208.

Darr, Katheryn Pfisterer. *Isaiah's Vision and the Family of God*. Literary Currents in Biblical Interpretation. Louisville: Westminster John Knox, 1994.

Day, Linda. "Rhetoric and Domestic Violence in Ezekiel 16." *Biblical Interpretation* 8 (2000) 205–30.

Day, Peggy L. "The Bitch Had It Coming to Her: Rhetoric and Interpretation in Ezekiel 16." *Biblical Interpretation* 8 (2000) 231–54.

Dearman, J. Andrew. "Daughter Zion and Her Place in God's Household." *Horizons in Biblical Theology* 31 (2009) 144–59.

DeRoche, Michael. "Jeremiah 2:2-3 and Israel's Love for God During the Wilderness Wanderings." *Concordia Theological Quarterly* 45 (1983) 364–76.

DesCamp, Mary Therese. *Metaphor and Ideology:* Liber Antiquitatum Biblicarum *and Literary Methods Through a Cognitive Lens.* Biblical Interpretation Series 87. Leiden: Brill, 2014.

Dever, William G. *The Lives of Ordinary People in Ancient Israel.* Grand Rapids: Eerdmans, 2012.

Dille, Sarah J. *Mixing Metaphors: God As Mother and Father in Deutero-Isaiah.* Gender, Culture, Theory 13. London: Continuum, 2004.

Dudrey, Russ. "'Submit Yourselves to One Another': A Socio-Historical Look at the Household Code of Ephesians 5:15—6:9." *Restoration Quarterly* 41 (1999) 27–44.

Ekblad, Bob. *Reading the Bible with the Damned.* Louisville: Westminster John Knox, 2005.

Elshout, Bartel. "The Unique Relationship between the Father and the Son in the Gospel of John." *Puritan Reformed Journal* 3 (2011) 41–55.

Ermatinger, James W. *The World of Ancient Rome: A Daily Life Encyclopedia*, 2 vols. Santa Barbara: ABC-CLIO, 2015.

Ferguson, Everett. *Backgrounds of Early Christianity.* 3rd ed. Grand Rapids: Eerdmans, 2003.

Feuillet, André. "L'heure de la femme (Jn 16:21) et l'heure de la Mère de Jésus (Jn 19:25-27)." *Biblica* 47.1–3 (1966) 169–84; 361–80; 557–73.

Feyaerts, Kurt. *The Bible through Metaphor and Translation: A Cognitive Semantic Perspective.* New York: Lang, 2003.

Filtvedt, Ole Jakob. "The Transcendence and Visibility of the Father in the Gospel of John." *Zeitschrift für die neutestamentliche Wissenschaft* 108 (2017) 90–118.

Flynn, Shawn W. *Children in Ancient Israel: The Hebrew Bible and Mesopotamia in Comparative Perspective.* Oxford: Oxford University Press, 2018.

Flynn, Shawn W., ed. *Children in the Bible and the Ancient World: Comparative and Historical Methods in Reading Ancient Children.* London: Routledge, 2019.

Follis, Elaine R. "Zion, Daughter of." In *ABD* 6:1103.

Fretheim, Terence E., and Beverly Roberts Gaventa, eds. *The Child in the Bible.* Grand Rapids: Eerdmans, 2008.

Garland, David E. "Severe Trials, Good Gifts, and Pure Religion: James 1." *Review & Expositor* 83 (1986) 383–94.

Garrett, Duane A. *Hosea, Joel*. New American Commentary 19A. Nashville: Broadman & Holman, 1997.

Garroway, Kristine, and John Martens, eds. *Children and Methods: Listening to and Learning from Children in the Biblical World*. Leiden: Brill, 2020.

Gillmayr-Bucher, Susanne. "Body Images in the Psalms." *Journal for the Study of the Old Testament* 28 (2004) 301–26.

Globe, Alexander. "Some Doctrinal Variants in Matthew 1 and Luke 2, and the Authority of the Neutral Text." *Catholic Biblical Quarterly* 42 (1980) 52–72.

Goodrich, John K. *Paul as an Administrator of God in 1 Corinthians*. Society for New Testament Studies Monograph Series 152. Cambridge: Cambridge University Press, 2012.

Goswell, Gregory. "What Makes the Arrangement of God with David in 2 Samuel 7 a Covenant?" *Restoration Quarterly* 60 (2018) 87–97.

Grassi, Joseph A. "Abba, Father (Mark 14:36): Another Approach." *Journal of the American Academy of Religion* 50 (1982) 449–58.

Greenberg, Moshe. *Ezekiel 21–37*. Anchor Bible 22A. New York: Doubleday, 1997.

Gundry, Judith M. "Children in the Gospel of Mark, with Special Attention to Jesus' Blessing of the Children (Mark 10:13-16) and the Purpose of Mark." In *The Child in the Bible*, edited by Terence E. Fretheim and Beverly Roberts Gaventa, 143–76. Grand Rapids: Eerdmans, 2008.

Gundry, Robert H. "In My Father's House are Many *Monai* (John 14:2)." *Zeitschrift für die neutestamentliche Wissenschaft* 58 (1967) 68–72.

Gunkel, Herman, and Joachim Begrich. *Introduction to the Psalms: The Genres of the Religious Lyric of Israel*. Translated by James D. Nogalski. Mercer Library of Biblical Studies. Macon, GA: Mercer University Press, 1998.

Haag, Istvan, et al. "Ezekiel 16 and Its Use of Allegory and the Disclosure-of-Abomination Formula." *Vetus Testamentum* 62 (2012) 198–210.

Hafemann, Scott J., and Paul R. House, eds. *Central Themes in Biblical Theology: Mapping Unity in Diversity*. Grand Rapids: Baker Academic, 2007.

"Hague Visa Process." https://travel.state.gov/content/travel/en/Intercountry-Adoption/Adoption-Process/immigrant-visa-process/us-hague-convention-adoption-and-visa-process.html.

Halter, Hugh. *Sacrilege: Finding Life in the Unorthodox Ways of Jesus*. Grand Rapids: Baker, 2011.

Hampe, Beate. "Embodiment and Discourse: Dimensions and Dynamics of Contemporary Metaphor Theory." In *Metaphor: Embodied Cognition and Discourse*, edited by Beate Hampe, 3–23. Cambridge: Cambridge University Press, 2017.

Heim, Erin M. *Adoption in Galatians and Romans: Contemporary Metaphor Theories and the Pauline* Huiothesia *Metaphors*. Biblical Interpretation Series 153. Leiden: Brill, 2017.

Hess, Ronald S. "Equality With and Without Innocence." In *Discovering Biblical Equality: Complementarity without Hierarchy*, edited by Ronald

W. Pierce and Rebecca Merrill Groothuis, 79–95. Downers Grove, IL: IVP Academic, 2005.

Hoezee, Scott. "'Live!': A Sermon on Ezekiel 16." *Calvin Theological Journal* 52 (2017) 85–91.

Horowitz, Maryanne Cline. "The Image of God in Man—Is Woman Included?" *Harvard Theological Review* 72 (1979) 175–206.

Howard-Brook, Wes. *Becoming Children of God: John's Gospel and Radical Discipleship*. Eugene, OR: Wipf & Stock, 2003.

Jacobs, Mignon R. "Ezekiel 16—Shared Memory of Yhwh's Relationship with Jerusalem: A Story of Fraught Expectations." In *Daughter Zion: Her Portrait, Her Response*, edited by Mark J. Boda et al., 201–23. Ancient Israel and Its Literature 13. Atlanta: Society of Biblical Literature, 2012.

Johnson, Elisabeth Ann. "Waiting for Adoption: Reflections on Romans 8:12–25." *Word & World* 22 (2002) 308–12.

Kaiser, Walter C., Jr. *The Promise-Plan of God: A Biblical Theology of the Old and New Testaments*. Grand Rapids: Zondervan: 2008.

Kalmanofsky, Amy. "The Dangerous Sisters of Jeremiah and Ezekiel." *Journal of Biblical Literature* 130 (2011) 299–312.

Keiser, Thomas A. "The Divine Plural: A Literary-Contextual Argument for Plurality in the Godhead." *Journal for the Study of the Old Testament* 34 (2009) 131–46.

Keller, Timothy. *Generous Justice: How God's Grace Makes Us Just*. New York: Penguin, 2010.

Kingsbury, Jack Dean. "The Title 'Son of David' in Matthew's Gospel." *Journal of Biblical Literature* 95 (1976) 591–602.

———. "Title Son of Man in Matthew's Gospel." *Catholic Biblical Quarterly* 37 (1975) 193–202.

Kirk, J. R. Daniel. "Appointed Son(s): An Exegetical Note on Romans 1:4 and 8:29." *Bulletin for Biblical Research* 14 (2004) 241–42.

Klink, Edward W., III, and Darian R. Lockett, eds. *Understanding Biblical Theology: A Comparison of Theory and Practice*. Grand Rapids: Zondervan Academic, 2012.

Knafl, Anne K. *Forming God: Divine Anthropomorphism in the Pentateuch*. Siphrut 12. Winona Lake, IN: Eisenbrauns, 2014.

Koller, Aaron. "Pornography or Theology? The Legal Background, Psychological Realism, and Theological Import of Ezekiel 16." *Catholic Biblical Quarterly* 79 (2017) 402–21.

Koskenniemi, Erkki. *The Exposure of Infants Among Jews and Christians in Antiquity*. Social World of Biblical Antiquity 2.4. Sheffield: Phoenix, 2009.

Kövecses, Zoltán. "Conceptual Metaphor Theory." In *The Routledge Handbook of Metaphor and Language*, edited by Elena Semino and Zsófia Demjén, 13–27. London: Routledge, 2017.

Kuhn, Karl A. "The 'One Like a Son of Man' Becomes the 'Son of God.'" *Catholic Biblical Quarterly* 69 (2007) 22–42.

Ladd, George Eldon. *The Gospel of the Kingdom*. Grand Rapids: Eerdmans, 1981.

Lakoff, George, and Mark Johnson. *Metaphors We Live By*. Chicago: Chicago University Press, 1980.

Lassen, Eva Maria. "The Use of the Father Image in Imperial Propaganda and 1 Corinthians 4:14-21." *Tyndale Bulletin* 42 (1991) 127–36.

Lewis, Robert Brian. *Paul's 'Spirit of Adoption' in Its Roman Imperial Context*. Library of New Testament Studies 545. London: Bloomsbury, 2016.

Levenson, Jon D. "Zion Traditions." In *ABD* 6:1098–102.

Levin, Yigal. "Jesus, 'Son of God' and 'Son of David': The 'Adoption' of Jesus into the Davidic Line." *Journal for the Study of the New Testament* 28 (2006) 415–42.

Levine, Amy-Jill, ed. *Feminist Companion to John*. Vol. 1. Feminist Companion to the New Testament and Early Christian Writings 4. London: Sheffield Academic, 2003.

Livingston, Gretchen. "About One-third of U.S. Children are Living with an Unmarried Parent." https://www.pewresearch.org/fact-tank/2018/04/27/about-one-third-of-u-s-children-are-living-with-an-unmarried-parent/.

Lockwood, Christopher. "Spiritual Fatherhood after the Model of Christ in the Gospel according to John." *Greek Orthodox Theological Review* 59 (2014) 81–127.

Løland, Hanne. *Silent Or Salient Gender? The Interpretation of Gendered God-language in the Hebrew Bible, Exemplified in Isaiah 42, 46, and 49*. Forschungen zum Alten Testament 2/32. Tübingen: Mohr Siebeck, 2008.

Longenecker, Richard N. "The Metaphor of Adoption in Paul's Letters." *The Covenant Quarterly* 72 (2014) 71–78.

Lyall, Francis. "Roman Law in the Writings of Paul." *Tyndale Bulletin* 32 (1981) 79–95.

Maier, Christl M. *Daughter Zion, Mother Zion: Gender, Space, and the Sacred in Ancient Israel*. Minneapolis: Fortress, 2008.

"The Majority of Children Live with Two Parents, Census Bureau Reports." https://www.census.gov/newsroom/press-releases/2016/cb16-192.html.

Malul, Meir. "Adoption of Foundlings in the Bible and Mesopotamian Documents: A Study of some Legal Metaphors in Ezekiel 16:1-7." *Journal for the Study of the Old Testament* 15 (1990) 97–126.

Mare, W. Harold. "Zion." In *ABD* 6:1096–7.

Martens, Elmer A. "The People of God." In *Central Themes in Biblical Theology: Mapping Unity in Diversity*, edited by Scott J. Hafemann and Paul R. House, 225–53. Grand Rapids: Baker Academic, 2007.

Mays, James Luther. *Hosea: A Commentary*. Old Testament Library. Philadelphia: Westminster, 1969.

McDowell, Catherine L. *The Image of God in the Garden of Eden: The Creation of Humankind in Genesis 2:5–3:24 in Light of the mīs pî pīt pî and wpt-r Rituals of Mesopotamia and Ancient Egypt*. Siphrut 15. Winona Lake, IN: Eisenbrauns, 2015.

McKnight, Scot. *The Jesus Creed: Loving God, Loving Others*. Brewster, MA: Paraclete, 2004.

McGregor Wright, R. K. "God, Metaphor and Gender: Is the God of the Bible a Male Deity?" In *Discovering Biblical Equality: Complementarity without Hierarchy*, edited by Ronald W. Pierce and Rebecca Merrill Groothuis, 287–300. Downers Grove, IL: IVP Academic, 2005.

Mead, James K. *Biblical Theology: Issues, Methods, and Themes*. Louisville: Westminster John Knox, 2007.

Meadowcroft, Tim. "'One Like a Son of Man' in the Court of the Foreign King: Daniel 7 as Pointer to Wise Participation in the Divine Life." *Journal for Theological Interpretation* 10 (2016) 245–63.

Meehan, Bridget Mary. *Delighting in the Feminine Divine*. Kansas City, MO: Sheed & Ward, 1994.

Melnyk, Janet L. R. "When Israel Was a Child: Ancient Near Eastern Adoption Formulas and the Relationship between God and Israel." In *History and Interpretation: Essays in Honour of John H. Hayes*, edited by M. Patrick Graham et al., 245–59. Journal for the Study of Old Testament Supplement 173. Sheffield: JSOT Press, 1993.

Metzger, Bruce M. *The Canon of the New Testament: Its Origin, Development, and Significance*. Oxford: Oxford University Press, 1989.

Michaelis, W. "μιμέομαι κλη." In *TDNT* 4:659–74.

Miller, John W. *Biblical Faith and Fathering: Why We Call God "Father."* Mahwah, NJ: Paulist, 1989.

Mitton, C. Leslie. *The Epistle to the Ephesians: Its Authorship, Origin and Purpose*. Eugene, OR: Wipf & Stock, 2002.

Mollenkott, Virginia Ramey. *The Divine Feminine: The Biblical Imagery of God as Female*. New York: Crossroads, 1984.

Moor, Johannes C. de. "The Duality in God and Man: Gen 1.26–27 as P's Interpretation of the Yahwistic Creation Account." In *Intertextuality in Ugarit and Israel*, edited by Johannes C. de Moor, 112–26. Oudtestamentische Studiën 40. Leiden: Brill, 1998.

Niskanen, Paul. "Yhwh as Father, Redeemer, and Potter in Isaiah 63:7-64:11." *Catholic Biblical Quarterly* 68 (2006) 397–407.

Noble, Paul R. *The Canonical Approach: A Critical Reconstruction of the Hermeneutics of Brevard S. Childs*. Biblical Interpretation Series 16. Leiden: Brill, 1995.

Pennington, Jonathan T. *The Sermon on the Mount and Human Flourishing: A Theological Commentary*. Grand Rapids: Baker Academic, 2017.

Peppard, Michael, "Adopted and Begotten Sons of God: Paul and John on Divine Sonship." *Catholic Biblical Quarterly* 73 (2011) 92–110.

Plato. *Republic, Volume I: Books 1-5*. Edited and translated by Christopher Emlyn-Jones and William Preddy. Loeb Classical Library 237. Cambridge: Harvard University Press, 2013.

Platt, David. *Follow Me: A Call to Die, A Call to Live*. Carol Stream, IL: Tyndale, 2013.

Pressler, Carolyn. *The View of Women Found in the Deuteronomic Family Laws*, Beihefte zur Zeitschrift für die alttestamentliche Wissenschaft 213. Berlin: de Gruyter, 1993.

Reinhartz, Adele. "Introduction: 'Father' as Metaphor in the Fourth Gospel." *Semeia* 85 (1999) 1–10.

Römer, Thomas. "The Exodus Narrative According to the Priestly Document." In *The Strata of the Priestly Writings: Contemporary Debate and Future Directions*, edited by Sarah Shectman and Joel S. Baden, 157–74. Abhandlungen zur Theologie des Alten und Neuen Testaments 95. Zurich: TVZ, 2009.

Rossell, William H. "New Testament Adoption: Graeco-Roman or Semitic?" *Journal of Biblical Literature* 71 (1952) 233–34.

Russaw, Kimberly D. *Daughters in the Hebrew Bible*. New York: Lexington, 2018.

Sakenfeld, Katharine Doob. "The Problem of Divine Forgiveness in Numbers 14." *Catholic Biblical Quarterly* 37 (1975) 217–330.

Sampley, J. Paul, ed. *Paul in the Greco-Roman World: A Handbook*. London: Trinity Press International, 2003.

Sawyer, Deborah F. *God, Gender and the Bible*. London: Routledge, 2002.

Scott, James M. *Adoption as Sons of God: An Exegetical Investigation into the Background of υἱοθεσία in the Pauline Corpus*. Wissenschaftliche Untersuchungen zum Neuen Testament 2/48. Tübingen: Mohr, 1992.

———. "Jesus' Vision for the Restoration of Israel as the Basis for a Biblical Theology of the New Testament." In *Biblical Theology: Retrospect and Prospect*, edited by Scott J. Hafemann, 129–43. Downers Grove, IL: InterVarsity, 2002.

Shead, Stephen. *Radical Frame Semantics and Biblical Hebrew: Exploring Lexical Semantics*. Biblical Interpretation Series 108. Leiden: Brill, 2014.

Shelley, Bruce L. *Church History in Plain Language*. 4th ed. Nashville: Nelson, 2013.

Shields, Mary E. "Multiple Exposures: Body Rhetoric and Gender Characterization in Ezekiel 16." *Journal of Feminist Studies in Religion* 14 (1998) 5–18.

Smith, Mark S. "The Heart and Innards in Israelite Emotional Expressions: Notes from Anthropology and Psychology." *Journal of Biblical Literature* 117 (1998) 427–36.

Smith, Paul R. *Is It Okay to Call God "Mother": Considering the Feminine Face of God*. Peabody, MA: Hendrickson, 1993.

Smoak, Jeremy D. *The Priestly Blessing in Inscription and Scripture: The Early History of Numbers 6:24-26*. Oxford: Oxford University Press, 2015.

Sneed, Mark. "Israelite Concern for the Alien, Orphan, and Widow: Altruism or Ideology?" *Zeitschrift für die alttestamentliche Wissenschaft* 111 (1999) 498–507.

Soards, Marion L. "Tradition, Composition, and Theology in Jesus' Speech to the 'Daughters of Jerusalem' (Luke 23:26-32)." *Biblica* 68 (1987) 221–44.

Soskice, Janet Martin. *The Kindness of God: Metaphor, Gender, and Religious Language*. Oxford: Oxford University Press, 2007.

Stiebert, Johanna. *Fathers and Daughters in the Bible*. Oxford: Oxford University Press, 2013.

Stuart, Douglas K. *Exodus*. New American Commentary 2. Nashville: Broadman & Holman, 2006.

Suzuki, Wendy. "The Brain-changing Benefits of Exercise?" https://www.ted.com/talks/wendy_suzuki_the_brain_changing_benefits_of_exercise?language=en#t-51677.

Sweetser, Eve, and Mary Therese DesCamp. "Motivating Biblical Metaphors for God: Refining the Cognitive Model." In *Cognitive Linguistic Explorations in Biblical Studies*, edited by Bonnie Howe and Joel B. Green, 7–23. Berlin: de Gruyter, 2014.

Thatcher, Adrian. *God, Sex, and Gender: An Introduction*. Hoboken, NJ: Wiley-Blackwell, 2011.

Tigay, Jeffery H. *Deuteronomy*. Jewish Publication Society Torah Commentary. Philadelphia: The Jewish Publication Society, 1996.

Trible, Phyllis. "Depatriarchalizing in Biblical Interpretation." *Journal of the American Academy of Religion* 41 (1973) 30–48.

Vanderstelt, Jeff. *Gospel Fluency: Speaking the Truths of Jesus into the Everyday Stuff of Life*. Wheaton, IL: Crossway, 2017.

Vellanickal, Matthew. *The Divine Sonship of Christians in the Johannine Writings*. Analecta Biblica 72. Rome: Biblical Institute Press, 1977.

Verner, David C. *The Household of God: The Social World of the Pastoral Epistles*, Society of Biblical Literature Dissertation Series 71. Chico, CA: Scholars, 1983.

Vos, Geerhardus. *Biblical Theology: Old and New Testaments*. Grand Rapids: Eerdmans, 1948.

Walker, Norman. "New Interpretation of the Divine Name Shaddai." *Zeitschrift für die alttestamentliche Wissenschaft* 72 (1960) 64–66.

Walsh, C., and M. W. Elliott, eds. *Biblical Theology: Past, Present, and Future*. Eugene, OR: Wipf & Stock, 2016.

Walters, James C. "Paul, Adoption, and Inheritance." In *Paul in the Greco-Roman World: A Handbook*, edited by J. Paul Sampley, 42–76. London: Trinity Press International, 2003.

Watt, Jan G. van der. *Family of the King: Dynamics of Metaphor in the Gospel according to John*. Biblical Interpretation Series 47. Leiden: Brill, 2000.

Wells, Jo Bailey. *God's Holy People: A Theme in Biblical Theology*. Journal for the Study of Old Testament Supplement 305. Sheffield: Sheffield Academic Press, 2000.

White, L. Michael. "Paul and *Pater Familias*." In *Paul in the Greco-Roman World: A Handbook*, edited by J. Paul Sampley, 457–87. London: Trinity Press International, 2003.

Widdicombe, Peter. "The Fathers on the Father in the Gospel of John." *Semeia* 85 (1999) 105–25.

Wijk-Bos, Johanna W. H. van. *Reimagining God: The Case for Scriptural Diversity*. Louisville: Westminster John Knox, 1995.

Wilkins, Michael J. "Imitate, Imitators." In *ABD* 3:392.

Witherington, Ben, III. *Conflict and Community in Corinth: A Socio-Rhetorical Commentary on 1 and 2 Corinthians*. Grand Rapids: Eerdmans, 1995.

Wright, Christopher J. H. *Knowing God the Father through the Old Testament*. Downers Grove, IL: IVP Academic, 2007.

Wright, N. T. *How God Became King: The Forgotten Story of the Gospels*. San Francisco: HarperOne, 2012.

———. *Simply Jesus: A New Vision of Who He Was, What He Did, and Why He Matters*. San Francisco: HarperOne, 2011.

———. *Surprised By Hope: Rethinking Heaven, The Resurrection, and The Mission of the Church*. San Fransisco: HarperOne, 2008.

Zoutewdaw, Erin Risch. "A Grotesque Attack: Reading Ezekiel 16 as Satire to Address Feminist Critiques." *Calvin Theological Journal* 52 (2017) 63–84.

Scripture Index

OLD TESTAMENT

Genesis

Exodus

Exodus (*continued*)

Leviticus

Deuteronomy

www.ingramcontent.com/pod-product-compliance
Lightning Source LLC
Chambersburg PA
CBHW070457090426
42735CB00012B/2593
* 9 7 8 1 7 2 5 2 6 7 6 2 6 *